W9-AYO-216

Link It!

Link It!

Colorful Chain Mail Jewelry
with Rubber O-Rings

Susan C. Thomas

LARK BOOKS

A Division of Sterling Publishing Co., Inc.
New York / London

Senior Editor: Terry Taylor

Editor: Larry Shea

Assistant Editor: Mark Bloom

Art Director: Dana Irwin

Design Assistant: Avery Johnson

Photographers: Steve Mann, Stewart O'Shields

Cover Designer: Cindy LaBreacht

Library of Congress Cataloging-in-Publication Data

Thomas, Susan C., 1959-
  Link It! : Colorful chain mail jewelry rubber o-rings / Susan C. Thomas. -- 1st ed.
     p. cm.
  Includes bibliographical references and index.
  ISBN-13: 978-1-60059-156-3 (pb-trade pbk. : alk. paper)
  ISBN-10: 1-60059-156-6 (pb-trade pbk. : alk. paper)
 1. Jewelry making. 2. Metal-work. 3. Chains (Jewelry) I. Title.
 TT212.T56 2008
 739.27--dc22

                                    2007047232

10 9 8 7 6 5 4 3 2 1

First Edition

Published by Lark Books, A Division of
Sterling Publishing Co., Inc.
387 Park Avenue South, New York, NY 10016

Text © 2008, Susan C. Thomas
Photography © 2008, Lark Books

Distributed in Canada by Sterling Publishing,
c/o Canadian Manda Group, 165 Dufferin Street
Toronto, Ontario, Canada M6K 3H6

Distributed in the United Kingdom by GMC Distribution Services,
Castle Place, 166 High Street, Lewes, East Sussex, England BN7 1XU

Distributed in Australia by Capricorn Link (Australia) Pty Ltd.,
P.O. Box 704, Windsor, NSW 2756 Australia

If you have questions or comments about this book, please contact:
Lark Books
67 Broadway
Asheville, NC 28801
828-253-0467

Manufactured in China

ISBN 13: 978-1-60059-156-3

For information about custom editions, special sales, premium
and corporate purchases, please contact Sterling Special Sales
Department at 800-805-5489 or specialsales@sterlingpub.com.

contents

introduction

This is not medieval chain mail made with thousands of interlocked steel rings. It's a brand-new way of making jewelry, using colorful new materials to create innovative textures and intricate designs.

Modern chain mail designs for jewelry call for rings that are more comfortable to wear—silver, stainless steel, rubber, or neoprene. I began working with aluminum and rubber rings, replicating the traditional weaves. Then I started experimenting with more and more rubber rings. How many could I include in one piece? How could I connect them all? The answer was surprisingly simple: with jump rings, of course! That settled, I was on my way.

When people see the jewelry I've made in this style, the question I'm asked most often is simply this: "Where did you come up with this stuff?" My answer is that this type of jewelry derives from a little imagination and many hours of trial and error.

An art teacher for the past 20 years, I've learned from students there is no single right way to create. All the rules in art can, will, should, and must be broken! "Look beyond the obvious," I tell my students. "Don't settle for your first or even your second idea. Keep thinking, looking, and experimenting to make your creation unique."

By manipulating the geometric shape of a rubber ring, I designed what I coined "the three basic elements." One basic element was triangular, which stumped me. What kind of jewelry is triangular? Then I remembered introducing my printmaking students to the works of M.C. Escher, and I knew I could tessellate any triangle into a rectangle.

As I experimented, I combined the basic elements into groups called units. From there, it was an easy matter to cold-connect units into a chain. Patterns emerged. Beginning with simple designs, the basic elements evolved to become the foundations for the colorful and varied bracelets, necklaces, and earrings you'll find in this book.

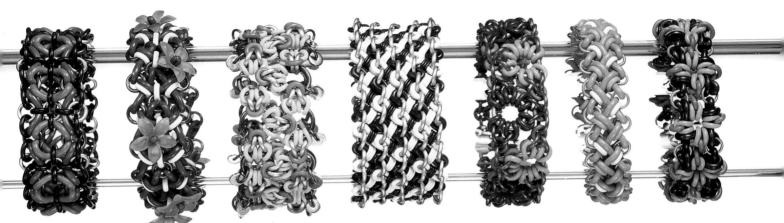

After you read the Basics section that follows and then begin dipping into the book's jewelry projects, two things will stand out. First, you'll notice that this jewelry requires only a few tools—pliers, scissors, and a ruler. Buy some inexpensive rubber or neoprene O-rings and metal jump rings, and you're ready to go. A number of projects also incorporate beads and various jewelry findings to add even more visual interest.

The second thing you'll happily discover is this: Once you've mastered the patterns of the three basic elements, you'll find every piece of jewelry here is really easy to make. These chain mail pieces offer a combination of qualities that are sure to please any jewelry maker: They're intricate in appearance, but simple in construction . . . or as I like to think of it—more compliments, less work.

Brilliant color combinations (Golden Crosses bracelet on page 69), interesting shapes (Bellflowers earrings on page 64), and intricate designs (Bright Blossom Necklace on page 90) are all showcased in the jewelry presented

here. Some pieces are timeless, some are more personal, but all have style and panache. They will delight you and your friends.

Just as I experimented to develop this type of jewelry, I urge you to experiment in creating your own pieces. Each piece looks and feels substantially different when made in different colors. So change colors. Change sizes. Add beads and other elements. Remember, you're creating art. All the rules can, will, should, and must be broken!

basics

Y ou've probably taken the opportunity to thumb through this book, in which case you've already seen much of the creative jewelry that you can make. Whether you're looking for a simple piece or something quite complex, there are necklaces, bracelets, and earrings here for everyone—from the beginning jewelry maker to the true expert.

Before you jump into your first project, however, take a few minutes to read through this section. It'll help you understand how to select and use the materials and tools that are called for in the projects. Most importantly, pages 20 to 24 describe how to combine jump rings and O-rings to make Basic Elements #1, #2, and #3, which are the building blocks for all of the jewelry in this book.

Materials

The exciting projects within the pages of this book use jump rings and O-rings: small rings made of rubber or neoprene. The O-rings give the jewelry an edgy, fun—sometimes sophisticated, sometimes frivolous—look, and they bring a unique, stretchy quality to the pieces as well.

The concept behind combining O-rings to make jewelry is simple: you can interconnect them in a variety of ways, including weaving, and then secure them with other O-rings or jump rings.

Jump Rings

Jump rings are affordable and made in a tremendous array of colors, sizes, and metals. You can buy them by weight or by the package. Anodized aluminum jump rings are the best choice for most of the beautiful jewelry you can make following the instructions in this book. Now all you need is an understanding of the size, gauge, and cut so that you can order your jump rings.

Ring Sizes

Jump ring dimensions are defined by the outer diameter (OD), inner diameter (ID), and gauge (g) or thickness. In a catalog or on packaging, you may see all three measurements—or just one or two. When all three numbers are provided, the first size listed is the OD. The ID is next, and the gauge is last. These measurements can be in metric (millimeters or mm) or inches.

Some jewelry suppliers don't provide the OD, but will give you the gauge. The number used to indicate gauge is counterintuitive: a smaller gauge number is a thicker wire. You need to pay attention to the gauge because a thick-gauge jump ring can be more difficult to handle, and while working with one you could mar the finish. A 14-gauge jump ring, for example, is attractive for jewelry, but it takes a firm grip to open and close the ring. A thicker 12-gauge jump ring is even more difficult to maneuver.

In this book, the lists of materials call for jump rings by the ID and the gauge—both in inches—as this is what you commonly find on websites and in catalogs.

Types of Jump Rings

You can make your own jump rings, but it's hardly worth the trouble, as commercially made ones are inexpensive and easy to purchase.

Commercially prepared rings are made by first coiling wire around a metal post or mandrel. Then the coil is cut to make the jump rings. Machine-cut rings are pinched, which creates a point-like seam. Saw-cut jump rings also start with a wire coiled around a mandrel, but the wire is cut with a saw. Machine-cut jump rings are a better choice because the cut edges don't snag clothing, and they're easier to close.

Neoprene or Rubber O-Rings

Every project in this book uses these stretchy rings, which are made from rubber or neoprene.

What makes O-rings so great for creating chain-mail jewelry is their flexibility. But, because the O-rings stiffen the usual fluidity of a chain, you might find that your finished jewelry could bunch up after it's worn a bit. If this happens, just tug the misshapen parts to bring them back in line.

O-rings are sold in a wide range of sizes, gauges, and colors, and are available from numerous sources (page 103). Some jewelry suppliers list the OD, ID, and then the gauge—usually in metric. Other sources offer only the ID and the gauge.

In this book, the lists of materials give O-ring measurements by the OD, the ID, and then the gauge. All of the measurements are in millimeters. For example, "15 x 10 x 2.5 mm" means the OD is 15 mm, the ID is 10 mm, and the gauge is 2.5 mm.

Beads

In the past, beads were not commonly included in chain mail jewelry. Designers usually found that exploring the hundreds of ways that the rings can be interconnected was more than enough to satisfy their creativity. Recently, though, more and more designers have begun embellishing their work with beads. To give you a chance to explore this trend, several projects in this book feature beads or bead caps (cuplike pieces that can be placed on the top or bottom of a bead, like a hat).

Many designers add beads to their chain mail jewelry by stringing them onto wire or cord and then feeding the length through the chain mail piece. But you can also add beads with some easier techniques that are used in the projects here.

For a flexible attachment, you can use a new technique that employs an O-ring to attach a bead. You need to carefully choose an O-ring size that fits snugly within the bead hole and won't easily pull out. For this technique, you need string. Waxed linen is the best choice because it won't cut through thinner rubber rings. A couple of the projects—including the Focal Star Bracelet (page 58) and Violet Bouquet (page 99)—use this technique.

Pay attention to the position of the hole, or drill, in the bead. You must use the drill that's noted in the project's materials list if you want to attach it as explained in the instructions. Here are the types of beads used for the projects in this book.

Center Drill—The hole goes through the center of the bead, from front to back.

Horizontal Drill—The hole travels from one side to the other, usually at the bead's midpoint.

Top Drill—The hole is positioned near the top of the bead.

Charm—The hole is created by a small loop above the top of the bead.

Jewelry Findings

These are metal components used within a piece of jewelry to attach and connect items. Findings include decorative rings, ear wires for earrings, and toggle clasps.

Other than a few toggles, you won't find many closures on the jewelry featured in this book. When it comes to the bracelets, clasps and other closers aren't required, thanks to the O-rings. Since O-rings are flexible and stretch, you can just slide the finished piece over your hand and onto your wrist.

When a project does require a finding, such as an ear wire for creating earrings, choose a finish that complements the color of your O-rings and jump rings. Anodized aluminum findings that will match the jump rings called for in most projects are hard to find, but this metal isn't your only choice. Your jewelry will look great if you plan ahead and adjust the color of your O-rings and jump rings to suit your own preferences.

Tools

One exciting advantage of making chain mail jewelry is that you only need a few basic tools to produce all the designs in this book: pliers, scissors, and a ruler. Naturally, you probably have scissors and a ruler—any will do. Here's some advice on the most suitable pliers.

Pliers

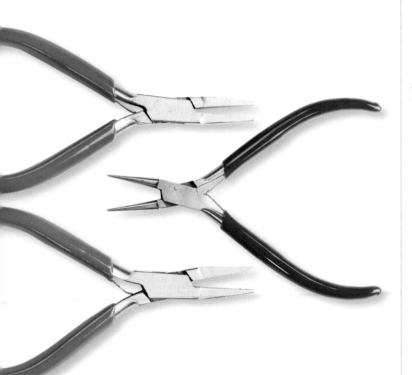

This tool (shown above) is void of any flat plane on the inside surfaces. Instead, they're round from the tip to the joint. The tips also range in size. A smaller tip is handy when the instructions for a project tell you to place three tiny (4.8 mm) O-rings over the end of the pliers. Avoid long round-nose pliers. They're more difficult to use with the techniques in this book.

You also need pliers that won't scratch or mar the jump rings. Flat-nose pliers (shown below) with a wide nose (¼ inch [6 mm]) give you extra control. Some even have slightly beveled edges inside the tips so that they won't cut into the surface of jump rings. If your favorite set of flat-nose pliers lacks bevels, sand the edges on both sides from the tips to the hinge.

To make most of the projects in this book you only need two flat-nose pliers and one pair of round-nose pliers. You'll use both of the flat-nose pliers to open and close jump rings (pages 16 to 18), and only one to lace items onto a jump ring.

You'll use the round-nose pliers to create two of the three building blocks, or basic elements (pages 20 to 24), that are part of many of the jewelry pieces. Round-nose pliers are the ideal tool for placing one O-ring onto another, as is the case when you make a Basic Element #1 (page 21).

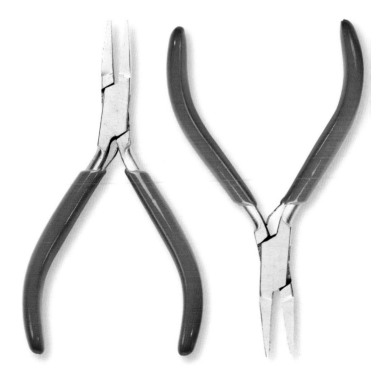

Alternatively, apply strong tape, such as reinforced packing tape, to the inside surface. To do this, cut a piece of tape into a rectangle that's large enough to wrap from the inside surface to the outside of a tip, with the tape ends overlapping on the outside. This isn't a permanent solution. The tape will eventually rip and wear off. In fact, if the tape tears off quickly, your grip on the pliers may be too tight. Relax a bit!

Start your collection by looking through your own tool-box. You may very well have some flat-nose pliers. Make sure they don't have teeth on the inside surface. It's best to use the type sold in craft and beading stores or at your favorite jewelry-maker supply store.

There are many brands of pliers—with various characteristics—on the market. Look for a style that fits nicely in your hand so that you'll experience less physical stress when you open and close multiple jump rings. Pliers that spring open easily, or even have adjustable spring bars, are preferable.

Techniques

You're sure to have a lot of fun creating and sharing this jewelry. If you haven't worked with jump rings, however, it's imperative that you have a clear understanding of the most basic concepts: opening and closing jump rings.

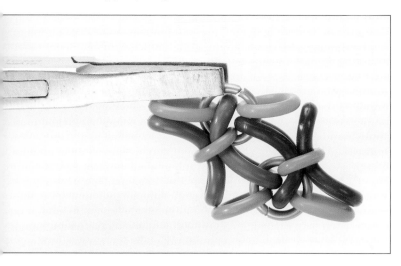

Commercially produced jump rings are packaged with the ends slightly opened. In order to lace or connect a jump ring, as instructed throughout the projects, you'll first have to open the jump ring enough to carry out the instructed step. You may even need to close a jump ring to proceed. The instructions always tell you what you need to do.

Your goal as you master opening and closing a ring is to protect the metal and maintain the circular shape of every jump ring, even though you're manipulating them. The instructions that follow will help you get a confident grip on these techniques.

You'll also find instructions here on how to lace jump rings, attach beads, and work with O-rings. The final part of this Basics section includes the step-by-step instructions and photos you need to follow to make the three basic elements that are the building blocks of every project.

Opening a Jump Ring

There's a specific technique to use for opening and closing jump rings. Learn it, love it, and don't try to change it. The objective is to ensure a round shape. An oval, deformed circle is clearly not attractive.

It's best to use two pair of flat-nose pliers to assure that you can open and close a jump ring without marring it. First you need to open the ring far enough that you can lace, or insert, it into another jump ring, O-ring, or bead. Open the ring too far and you'll run the risk of being unable to return it to its original shape: The ends won't line up.

1. Place one of the pliers in your hand with one handle against your palm, on the thumb muscle that extends down that far. Wrap your thumb around this handle. Grip the other handle with all four fingertips, just above the top joint (see the photo below). Squeeze with your four fingertips to open and close the jaws. Experiment with the hand you use. Some people find it easier to hold the jump ring in their dominant hand so they can hold the flat-nose pliers in their non-dominant hand.

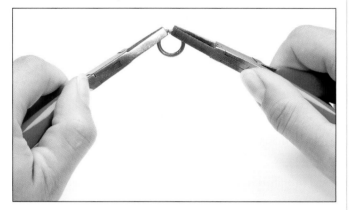

2. Pick up a jump ring with your fingers. Turn it so that the opening is at the top, in the center. Place the tip of the flat-nose pliers so that they cover up as much of the ring as possible, without going past the center of the circle, or above the top of the ring.

3. Pick up the second flat-nose pliers with your free hand, and situate this pair on the opposite side of the ring in the same manner.

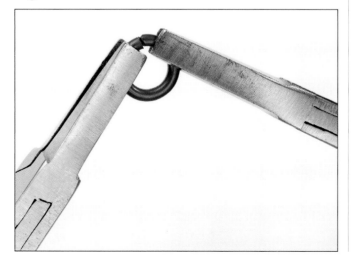

4. Bring the pliers in your dominant hand toward you. In other words, if you're right-handed, you should open the jump ring by shifting the left side of the jump ring away from you and bringing the right side closer to you. If your left hand is dominant, open the sides of the jump ring in the opposite manner. The part of the jump ring that actually bends is directly opposite the opening. Move both pliers equally, in opposite directions.

Always open jump rings in the same direction. This is important when you're lacing them (page 18). The only part of the ring that should bend is exactly opposite the opening. The part of the jump ring that's covered by the pliers, if you maintain your grip, shouldn't bend.

here are a few incorrect ways to hold your pliers while working on the projects in this book. You'll save yourself time and hand cramps if you learn to open and close jump rings the correct way.

Closing a Jump Ring

Once you've laced a jump ring through another item according to the specific step in a project, you need to close it unless otherwise instructed. (Some steps require you to do some additional actions before closing the jump ring.)

1. With both pliers in the correct positions described in steps 2 and 3 of Opening a Jump Ring (page 17), reverse the direction that you used to open them.

2. If you release the jump ring where the two ends meet, the metal will be in a less-than-perfect position. Therefore, it's necessary to condition the metal by going beyond where the ends of the jump ring would meet.

3. Move the ends back and forth—slightly and just a few times—so that the ends line up when the pliers are released. If they don't, repeat the conditioning.

Now practice opening and closing a few jump rings . . . it's very cool.

Several of the projects involve steps where you have to lace up to four O-rings onto a single open jump ring. This leaves a lot less space on the jump ring to get a firm grip with the pliers. Squish the rings together to create more jump ring surface so that you can close the pliers without marring the jump ring. Doing this successfully is the real test; it proves that you have the technique for closing jump rings mastered.

Lacing a Jump Ring

In many projects you're instructed to lace an open jump ring. This can be as easy as inserting one end of the jump ring through another closed ring. Other times, you need to lace a jump ring through a very tight spot. Here's some advice to ease the pain.

- Always lace a ring with it held in flat-nose pliers, in your dominant hand. You'll have to hold the ring, element, or unit with your other hand to keep it steady.

- Be aware of the motion and direction you need to use with a jump ring. Consider sewing with a needle: The needle is straight, so the length of the needle follows a straight path as it's inserted through the fabric. Now think about the shape of the jump ring: It's round. This means that you have to use a circular movement.

- You'll often lace a jump ring through the end of an O-ring—sometimes more than one at a time. Some of these ends will be sticking up so that they're easy to lace. Others are pulled or held tight against other O-rings. If you face both situations in one action, it's easiest to lace through the tightest space first and the loosest space second.

Jewelry Sizing

The most distinctive quality of the jewelry between the covers of this book is the intertwining of the O-rings. If you've ever handled an O-ring, you already know that it has some bounce and stretch. So, even though the jewelry projects are sized to fit an average person, the fit is forgiving. The bracelets are designed to fit an adult with a wrist circumference of 7½ inches (19 cm). The necklaces are 19 inches (48.3 cm) or longer.

If you desire a bracelet or necklace that's larger or smaller, you can adjust the fit. Each piece of jewelry consists of basic elements that are combined to make units. Then the units are combined to create the desired length of the finished piece. So adjusting the length is as simple as adding or subtracting one or more units. All of the project instructions tell you the point where you can consider adding more—or excluding—units or elements.

If you have large wrists, you could figure out the number of additional jump rings and O-rings before starting a project. But even if you do this, you'll probably end up buying the same amount of materials, because jump rings and O-rings are rarely sold individually.

Basic Elements

All the jewelry in this book starts with one of three basic units made from O-rings of different sizes and colors. The variation in the pieces stems from the way the basic elements interact—in other words, how you put them together, using jump rings or other elements. A quick scan of this book reveals a variety of patterns, each reproduced in one color combination, but you can change the colors of any piece, giving it a different, more personal, look. Master the three basic elements, and then you can experiment with a whole world of patterns and color!

Basic Element #1

This is the simplest of the three basic elements that form the foundation for the projects in this book. Basic Element #1 uses only two O-rings, so it's very easy to make. The process, which involves placing one O-ring through another, is referenced throughout this book.

Often, the instructions tell you to pull this basic element through the end of another basic element or O-ring. In this situation, only draw it through until the center O-ring on the element butts against the opening.

materials + tools

1 O-ring, 7 x 3 x 2 mm
1 O-ring, 15 x 10 x 2.5 mm
Round-nose pliers

instructions

1. Place the small O-ring over the tip of the round-nose pliers. If the project you're making features multiple small O-rings on a large one, mount all of them on the pliers. Hold onto the ring(s) with your index finger.

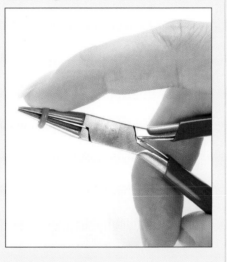

2. Open the pliers slightly. Don't overstretch the small ring(s). Push the end of the large O-ring into the open pliers, and close them tightly.

3. Flatten the large O-ring with your free hand, at the same time placing it in line with the pliers.

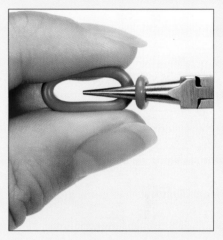

4. Pull the small O-ring(s) off the pliers and onto the center of the large O-ring. If you're working with more than one small O-ring, don't allow the small rings to overlap.

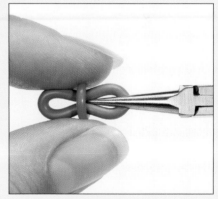

NOTE: The size and number of the O-rings used for this basic element may vary. Check the instructions for your project.

Basic Element #2

This element is just a bit more complicated than the first and has an entirely different appearance. But like the other two basic elements, you can use it in many creative ways.

materials + tools

2 O-rings, 12 x 8 x 2 mm

1 O-ring, 7 x 3 x 2 mm

1 anodized aluminum jump ring, 14-gauge, ⅜ inch

2 anodized aluminum jump rings, 16-gauge, ³⁄₁₆ inch

2 flat-nose pliers

NOTE: The size and number—and even the type—of O-rings used for this basic element may vary. Check the instructions for your project.

instructions

1. Open the two small jump rings and set them aside for use in steps 2 and 4. Use both flat-nose pliers for this process (pages 16 to 17). Hold the large jump ring in your non-dominant hand. Squeeze one of the large O-rings flat with your dominant hand, and insert it through the jump ring.

2. Fold the O-ring in half so that it's wrapped around the jump ring, holding the jump ring in place with the fingers of your non-dominant hand.

3. Grasp one of the open jump rings with a pair of flat-nose pliers held in your dominant hand. Lace the jump ring through both ends of the O-ring.

4. Lace the small O-ring onto the same open jump ring, still maintaining your grip on the flat-nose

pliers. Close the jump ring using both flat-nose pliers. The unit should now look like this.

5. Wrap the remaining large O-ring around the same large jump ring with your fingers. Secure the ends of this second large O-ring with the remaining small jump ring, using the flat-nose pliers.

6. Lace the same open jump ring through the same small O-ring you attached in step 3.

7. The unit should now look like this. Close the jump ring.

Basic Element #3

This element looks more complex than it really is. All you do is add another large O-ring to a Basic Element #1 (page 21). Basic Element #3 is beautiful enough to use on its own (as an earring, for example), but it also forms the foundation for even more creative shapes.

materials + tools

2 O-rings, 15 x 10 x 2.5 mm

1 O-ring, 7 x 3 x 2 mm

Round-nose pliers

NOTE: The size and number of the O-rings used for this basic element may vary. Check the instructions for your project. The two 15-mm O-rings can be the same color or different colors, as shown in this example.

instructions

1. Make a Basic Element #1 using one of the 15-mm O-rings, the 7-mm O-ring, and the round-nose pliers (page 21).

2. Insert the pliers through one end of the finished Basic Element #1 and out through the opposite end. Press against the Basic Element #1, and then hold it on the pliers with the index finger of the hand holding the pliers.

3. Squeeze the remaining 15-mm O-ring flat with your available hand, and firmly grasp the end of the loose O-ring between the tips of the pliers.

4. Pull the Basic Element #1 onto the 15-mm O-ring with the fingers of your left hand on top of and underneath the element. Pull it to the

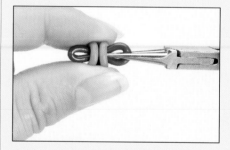

center of the 15-mm O-ring, making sure the 7-mm O-ring is centered and visible.

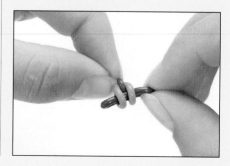

the projects

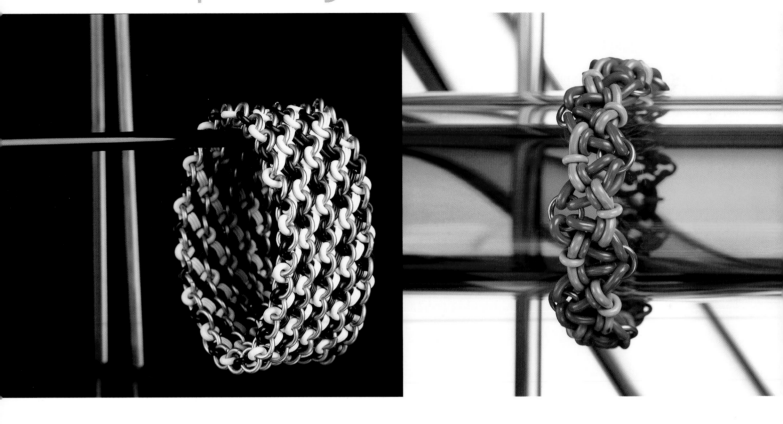

turquoise
ZIGZAG

Get a handle on the basic
techniques with this bracelet.
Experimenting with color
choices is also easy.

instructions

1 Using the round-nose pliers, create 32 basic elements, each with one purple 15-mm O-ring and one purple 7-mm O-ring (page 21). Make 16 additional basic elements with a turquoise 15-mm O-ring and an orange 7-mm O-ring.

2 Pinch the ends of one of the turquoise and orange elements between the thumb and forefinger of your dominant hand to force the element into a curved shape. Release the element. It'll hold its shape.

3 Insert the round-nose pliers through one free end of the curved element, from the outside of the curve to the inside, and pull the end of a purple element through.

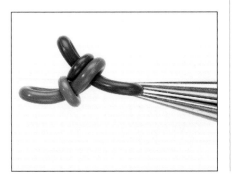

4 Insert the round-nose pliers through the remaining free end of the curved element, from the same side as in step 3. Pull the end of another purple element through. This is one unit.

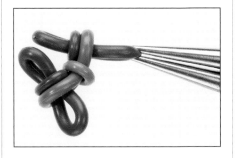

5 Create 15 additional units.

6 Lay the units side by side on a flat surface. Flip every other unit upside down.

7 Open a jump ring, using both flat-nose pliers (page 16). Lace the jump ring through the two free ends of the second unit, which come together like the point of a triangle. Lace the same open jump ring through the closest free end in each of the neighboring units. Close the jump ring, again using both flat-nose pliers.

materials + tools

32 purple O-rings, 15 x 10 x 2.5 mm

32 purple O-rings, 7 x 3 x 2 mm

16 turquoise O-rings, 15 x 10 x 2.5 mm

16 orange O-rings, 7 x 3 x 2 mm

16 purple 16-gauge anodized aluminum jump rings, ¼ inch

Round-nose pliers

Flat-nose pliers, 2 pair

BASIC ELEMENT #1

8 Add units in this manner—attaching them on alternating sides of the length—until you've joined all of them or the bracelet is the desired length.

9 Attach the beginning of the length to the end using two jump rings and the same method to connect the units. Rotate all of the jump rings to hide the cut ends.

triangles
BRACELET

Flip and flop simple triangles into a fun band. This project is great for beginners because it eases you into working with basic elements.

instructions

1 Create 36 basic elements, each with one 15-mm O-ring and one 7-mm O-ring, using the round-nose pliers (page 21).

2 Open an orange jump ring (page 16). Lace it through one end of each of two basic elements. Close the jump ring. Use both flat-nose pliers for this process and as needed in the following steps.

3 Open another orange jump ring, and lace it through the free end of one of the joined elements and one end of a third element. Close the jump ring.

4 Arrange the joined elements in a triangle so the center element has one loop underneath and one loop over the adjoining elements. Overlap the ends of the first and third element. Make sure all three

elements have one end under and the other end over the adjoining elements. Open another orange jump ring and lace it through the free ends of two elements to complete the triangle. Close the jump ring. This is one unit.

5 Create 11 additional units.

6 Lay the units side by side on a flat surface with every other unit upside down.

7 Open a black jump ring. Lace it through the closed jump ring in each of three neighboring units. Close the jump ring. Attach additional units to the joined ones in the same manner until you've joined all the units or until the bracelet is the desired length.

materials + tools

36 yellow O-rings, 15 x 10 x 2.5 mm

36 dark green O-rings, 7 x 3 x 2 mm

36 orange 16-gauge anodized aluminum jump rings, ³⁄₁₆ inch

12 black 16-gauge anodized aluminum jump rings, ³⁄₁₆ inch

Round-nose pliers

Flat-nose pliers, 2 pair

BASIC ELEMENT #1

8 Open the last two black jump rings. Join the beginning of the length to the end the same way you attached the previous units. Rotate all of the jump rings to hide the cut ends.

light & lively
EARRINGS

Here's a simple and quick project: making a pair or two of these earrings. They'll complement any of the bracelets in this book.

instructions

1 Create six basic elements, each with one 15-mm O-ring and one 7-mm O-ring (page 21). Use the round-nose pliers.

2 Using both flat-nose pliers, open a ³⁄₁₆-inch jump ring (page 16). Lace two basic elements onto the jump ring. Close the jump ring, using both pliers again.

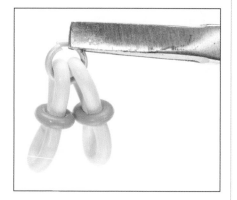

3 Open a ³⁄₁₆-inch jump ring. Lace it through the free end of one of the attached elements, plus the end of a third element. Close the jump ring.

4 Arrange the joined elements in a triangle. Overlap the ends of the first and third elements. Make sure all three elements have one end under and the other end over the adjoining element. Open another ³⁄₁₆-inch jump ring, and lace it through the free ends of two elements to complete the triangle. Close the jump ring. This is one unit.

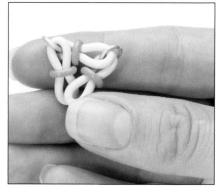

5 Create one additional unit.

6 Open a jump ring on one of the triangular units, and lace it through a 7-mm O-ring. Close the jump ring. Open a second jump ring on the same element, lace it through another 7-mm O-ring, and close the jump ring. Open two jump rings on the second triangular unit. Attach them to the 7-mm O-rings you just added to the first element. Close the jump rings.

7 Open the jump ring at the top (one pointed end) of one of the tri-angular units. Lace it through the loop on an earring post. Close the jump ring.

materials + tools

12 white O-rings, 15 x 10 x 2.5 mm

16 yellow O-rings, 7 x 3 x 2 mm

12 silver-color 18-gauge etched aluminum jump rings, ³⁄₁₆ inch

2 yellow 18-gauge anodized aluminum jump rings, ⁵⁄₃₂ inch

2 silver-plated earring posts

2 silver-color bead charms, 7 x 13 mm, with loops large enough to fit an 18-gauge ring

Round-nose pliers

Flat-nose pliers, 2 pair

BASIC ELEMENT #1

8 Open a ⁵⁄₃₂-inch jump ring. Lace it through the attached jump ring at the bottom of the triangular unit and the charm loop. Close the jump ring. Rotate all of the jump rings to hide the cut ends.

9 Repeat these instructions to make a matching second earring.

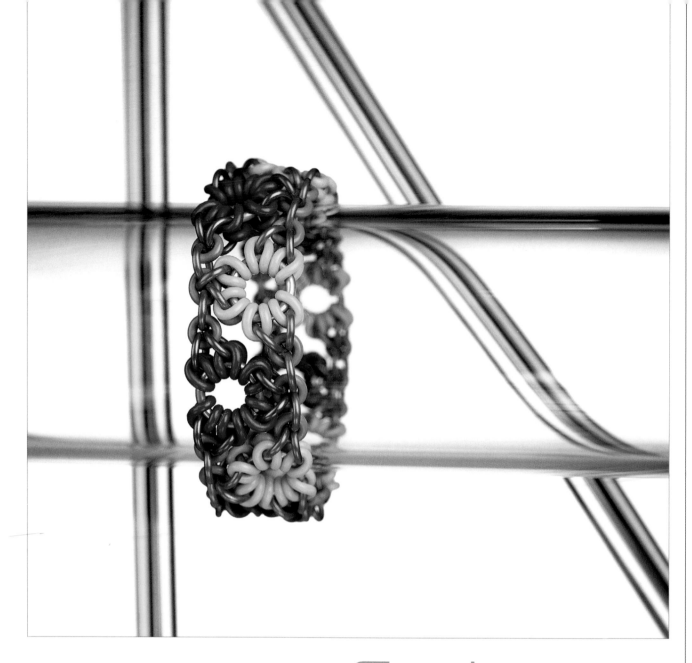

up & down
MOTIFS

In this floral bouquet, you make the flowers. The process isn't complex, so you can whip up this piece in no time.

instructions

1 Create one basic element using two of the yellow 12-mm O-rings, one of the 7-mm O-rings, and two of the violet ³⁄₁₆-inch jump rings on a ³⁄₈-inch jump ring (page 22). Use both flat-nose pliers for this process and as needed for the following steps (page 16). Close the ³⁄₈-inch jump ring.

2 Make two more basic elements on the same closed ³⁄₈-inch jump ring and using the same colors. This is one unit.

3 Create four additional units with the same colors. Create five more units using blue 12-mm O-rings, 7-mm O-rings, and purple ³⁄₁₆-inch jump rings onto ³⁄₈-inch jump rings.

4 Lay the units side by side on a flat surface, alternating the colors. Turn every second unit upside down. Open a violet ³⁄₁₆-inch jump ring. Lace it through the 7-mm O-rings of two neighboring units. Close the jump ring.

5 Open another violet ³⁄₁₆-inch jump ring. Lace it through another 7-mm O-ring on each of the same two triangular units.

6 Attach additional units until all are joined or the bracelet is the desired length.

7 Join the beginning of the length to the end by lacing two jump rings through the final two unattached 7-mm O-rings of the last and first unit. Rotate all of the jump rings to hide the cut ends.

materials + tools

30 yellow O-rings, 12 x 8 x 2 mm

30 turquoise O-rings, 7 x 3 x 2 mm

30 blue O-rings, 12 x 8 x 2 mm

50 violet 16-gauge anodized aluminum jump rings, ³⁄₁₆ inch

10 pink 14-gauge anodized aluminum jump rings, ³⁄₈ inch

30 purple 16-gauge anodized aluminum jump rings, ³⁄₁₆ inch

Flat-nose pliers, 2 pair

BASIC ELEMENT #2

double-crossed

Basic elements held tightly together give this bracelet a sturdy feel. The chunky jump rings complement the effect.

instructions

1 Make a basic element using the round-nose pliers: start with a 7-mm O-ring centered on a 12-mm O-ring, and then add a 15-mm O-ring (page 24). Create 39 additional basic elements in the same manner.

2 Insert the round-nose pliers through the end of one of the elements and pull one end of a second element through the end of the first. Position the 7-mm O-rings on the outside edge of the unit you're making.

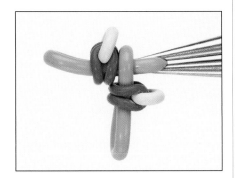

3 Insert the round-nose pliers through the opposite end of the second element and pull the end of the first element through the end of the second.

4 Grasp the two ends of the elements that extend from this unit, and pull on them to shape them evenly. This is one unit.

5 Create and shape 19 additional units.

6 Lay the units side by side on a flat surface. Rotate them so they're lined up in the same manner, with the free ends of the 15-mm O-rings almost vertical, pointing to the right at the top and to the left at the bottom.

materials + tools

40 white O-rings, 7 x 3 x 2 mm

40 red O-rings, 12 x 8 x 2 mm

40 yellow O-rings, 15 x 10 x 2.5 mm

40 red 14-gauge anodized aluminum jump rings, ¼ inch

Round-nose pliers

Flat-nose pliers, 2 pair

BASIC ELEMENT #3

7 Open a jump ring, using both flat-nose pliers for this process and as needed for the following steps (page 16). Starting at the right end of the arranged units, lace the jump ring through the overlapped end at the top of the second unit.

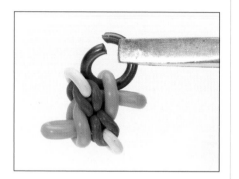

8 Lace the same open jump ring through the free end of an element in the first unit. This is the end you pulled out far; it's easy to lace. Close the jump ring.

9 Rotate the joined units, and attach the opposite sides of the units in the same manner.

10 Attach additional units in the same manner until all are joined or the bracelet is the desired length.

11 Join the beginning of the bracelet to the end in the same manner.

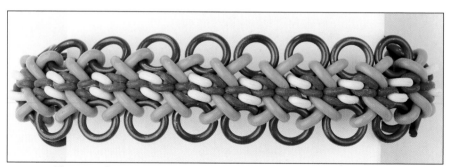

The negative space of the jump rings creates a dramatic contrast with the tightly woven weave.

bright
BANGLE

A small change can have exciting results. All you
have to do is tweak a basic element to come up
with the building blocks for this piece.

materials + tools

16 purple O-rings, 15 x 10 x 2.5 mm

16 yellow O-rings, 7 x 3 x 2 mm

16 green O-rings, 15 x 10 x 2.5 mm

32 yellow O-rings, 10 x 6 x 2 mm

32 16-gauge yellow anodized aluminum jump rings, ¼ inch

Round-nose pliers

Flat-nose pliers, 2 pair

BASIC ELEMENT #1

instructions

1 Using the round-nose pliers, create eight basic elements (page 21) with a variation, making each one with two purple 15-mm O-rings and one 7-mm O-ring. To do this, push the two large O-rings—not just one—into the open pliers that already hold the small O-ring. Create eight additional elements, also with a variation: Make each one with two green 15-mm O-rings and one 7-mm O-ring.

2 Open a jump ring using both flat-nose pliers for this process and as needed for the following steps (page 16). Lace the jump ring through the attached 7-mm O-ring and the shorter end of one of the 15-mm O-rings on one element. Also lace the jump ring through one of the 10-mm O-rings.

3 Lace the same open jump ring through the longer end of a second, green element, and through a second 10-mm O-ring. Close the jump ring.

4 Rotate the two joined elements and join the opposite ends in the same manner.

5 Open a jump ring. Join a new element in an alternate color. Lace the jump ring through the nearest attached 10-mm O-ring, and then lace the same jump ring through the attached element in the same manner as the previous steps. Now lace the jump ring through a free end in the new element, and finish by adding only one 10-mm O-ring. Rotate and join the opposite ends.

6 Attach additional elements in the same manner and alternating the colors until all of them are joined or the bracelet is the desired length.

7 Join the beginning of the length to the end in the same manner, without adding any 10-mm O-rings. Instead, open the last two jump rings. Lace them through the 10-mm O-rings attached to the first and last elements of the length, at both sides. Rotate all of the jump rings to hide the cut ends.

A fine adjustment to the basic element produces a weave wih character.

black
tie
AFFAIR

What turns a piece of jewelry from just plain fun into something sophisticated?

Here it's the colors, the weave, and some ceramic beads.

instructions

1 Create 121 basic elements, each with one white 12-mm O-ring and three 4.8-mm O-rings (page 21). Start each element by inserting a black, a white, and then a black 4.8-mm O-ring onto the tip of the round-nose pliers.

2 Insert the round-nose pliers through one end of an element (A) and pull one end of the second element (B) through the end of the first.

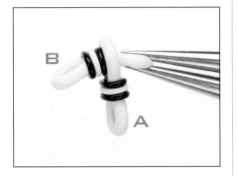

3 Insert the round-nose pliers through the free end of the element you just pulled through the O-ring (B). Pull one end of a new element (C) through the second element.

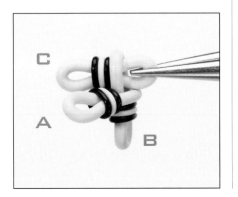

4 Open one of the ³⁄₁₆-inch jump rings using both of the flat-nose pliers for this process and as needed for the following steps (page 16). Lace the jump ring through the free ends of Elements A and B. Close the jump ring.

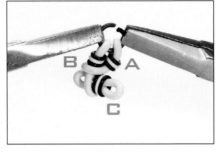

5 Open another ³⁄₁₆-inch jump ring. Lace it through the free end of Element C. Before closing the jump ring, also lace it through the three 4.8-mm O-rings on the first element.

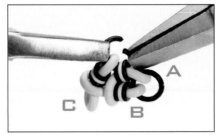

6 Insert the round-nose pliers through the end of element C, and pull one end of a fourth element (D) through the end of the other element.

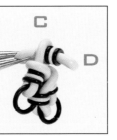

materials + tools

122 white O-rings, 12 x 8 x 2 mm

244 black O-rings, 4.8 x 2.8 x 1 mm

122 white O-rings, 4.8 x 2.8 x 1 mm

123 black 16-gauge anodized aluminum jump rings, ³⁄₁₆ inch

3 silver-color 16-gauge aluminum jump rings, ³⁄₈ inch

3 black and white center-drill, disk-shaped focal beads, 15 mm, with a hole large enough to fit a ³⁄₈-inch jump ring

Silver-plated toggle bar, 16 mm

Black O-ring, 12 x 8 x 2 mm

Round-nose pliers

Flat-nose pliers, 2 pair

BASIC ELEMENT #1

FOCAL BEADS BY JOAN MILLER

7 Open another ³⁄₁₆-inch jump ring, and lace it through the end of Element D that you didn't pull through Element C. Also lace the open jump ring through the attached end of the closest O-ring (Element A) and the neighboring three 4.8-mm O-rings that are part of Element B. Close the jump ring.

8 Attach additional elements in the same manner—adding another basic element and then attaching a jump ring at the opposite end-until you've joined all the elements or until the necklace is the desired length.

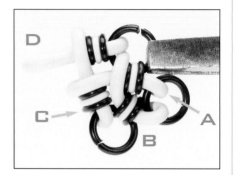

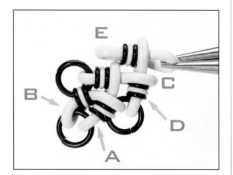

9 Open another ³⁄₁₆-inch jump ring. Lace it through the free end of the last element, the closest attached end of an O-ring, and the three 4.8-mm O-rings.

10 Open another ³⁄₁₆-inch jump ring. Lace it around—not through—the last O-ring you added. Also lace the open jump ring through the loop on the toggle bar. Close the jump ring.

11 Open all three of the ³⁄₈-inch jump rings. Lace one through each of the focal beads. Before closing the jump rings, lace each one onto the black 12-mm O-ring.

12 Open the jump ring at the beginning of the necklace (the end that doesn't hold the toggle bar), and lace it through the 12-mm O-ring with the three beads. Close the jump ring.

13 Lay the necklace on a flat surface. Press down on the edges to shape the piece. Rotate all the jump rings to hide the cut ends. To close the finished piece, insert the toggle, from back to front, through the black 12-mm O-ring at the opposite end.

basket weave
BLUES

A complicated bracelet is bound to turn heads. This one is a challenge, so develop your skills by making a few other projects before tackling it.

materials + tools

48 purple O-rings, 7 x 3 x 2 mm

48 blue O-rings, 15 x 10 x 2.5 mm

48 turquoise O-rings,
15 x 10 x 2.5 mm

48 white O-rings, 7 x 3 x 2 mm

48 dark green O-rings, 7 x 3 x 2 mm

24 violet 16-gauge anodized
aluminum jump rings, ³⁄₁₆ inch

48 blue 16-gauge anodized aluminum
jump rings, ³⁄₁₆ inch

Round-nose pliers

Flat-nose pliers, 2 pair

BASIC ELEMENT #3

instructions

1 Make a basic element starting with a purple 7-mm O-ring centered on a blue 15-mm O-ring. Then add a turquoise 15-mm O-ring (page 24). Create 47 additional basic elements in the same manner, always using the round-nose pliers.

2 Open a violet jump ring, using both flat-nose pliers (page 16). Lace it through a free end of one of the elements.

3 Lace the opposite end of the same O-ring through the same jump ring. The 7-mm O-ring is in the center of the turquoise element. Squeeze the folded element close to the flat-nose pliers while keeping a firm grip on the ring.

4 Lace the same jump ring through both free ends of another basic element. Force over the second element so you can close the jump ring.

5 Arrange the two elements on opposite sides of the jump ring. If necessary, move the 7-mm O-rings so both basic elements are symmetrical, as shown in the photo. This is one unit.

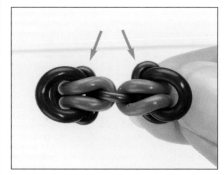

6 Create 23 additional units.

7 Insert the round-nose pliers through the end of a 15-mm O-ring in the first unit. Grasp the protruding end of a 15-mm O-ring in a second unit. Pull the top of the O-ring in the second unit through the first.

8 Open a blue jump ring. Flip the two units. Lace the jump ring through the end of the O-ring in the second unit, which you previously pulled through.

9 Lace four 7-mm O-rings onto the same open jump ring beginning with a white on both sides of the jump ring, and then a dark green on both sides. Close the jump ring.

10 Rotate the joined units to attach the neighboring sides at the bottom. Lace four 7-mm O-rings onto a new open jump ring in the same order as in step 9. Close the jump ring.

11 Pull through the protruding end of an O-ring at the top of a third unit. Open a blue jump ring, and lace it through the closest dark green and white O-rings, in that order. Lace the same jump ring through the end of the third unit you just pulled through, and then add a white O-ring and a dark green O-ring. Close the jump ring. Join the bottom of the third unit in the same manner.

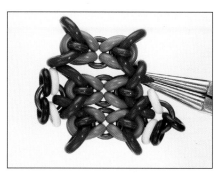

12 Attach additional units until you've joined them all or until the bracelet is the desired length.

13 Attach the beginning of the length to the end in the same manner, but don't add any new 7-mm O-rings. Instead, lace the open jump ring through the two attached 7-mm O-rings at each edge. Repeat this process at the bottom. Rotate all of the jump rings to hide the cut ends.

rays
OF SUNSHINE

Start with the three elements that form the Triangles Bracelet (page 30). Add another, and you've got the four-unit shape that's the foundation of this piece.

instructions

1 Using the round-nose pliers, create 56 basic elements, each with one 15-mm O-ring and one 7-mm O-ring (page 21).

2 Insert the round-nose pliers through the end of one of the elements, and pull one end of a second element through.

3 Insert the round-nose pliers through the end of the second element. Pull a third element through.

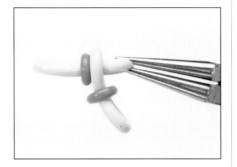

4 Insert the round-nose pliers through the end of the third element. Pull a fourth element through.

5 Insert the round-nose pliers through the end of the fourth element and pull the first element through. This is one unit.

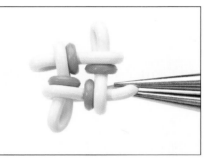

6 Create 13 additional units.

7 Lay all of the square units side by side. Make sure all the free ends and overlapping ends of the O-rings are oriented in the same manner. The next step will be easier if they're oriented as shown in the photo below.

materials + tools

56 white O-rings, 15 x 10 x 2.5 mm

56 yellow O-rings, 7 x 3 x 2 mm

28 bronze-color 16-gauge anodized aluminum jump rings, ¼ inch

Round-nose pliers

Flat-nose pliers, 2 pair

BASIC ELEMENT #1

8 Open a jump ring, using both flat-nose pliers (page 16). Lace the jump ring through the attached end of an element in a unit and the O-ring that's next to it. Lace the same open jump ring through the free end of the element to the left.

9 Lace the same open jump ring through a free end of an O-ring in a second unit. Close the jump ring, again using both flat-nose pliers (page 18).

10 Open a jump ring. Lace it through the opposite side of the two units, repeating steps 8 and 9.

11 Add more units in the same manner, repeating steps 8 to 10, until you've joined all of the units or the bracelet is the desired length.

12 Join the beginning of the length to the end in the same manner, using the last two jump rings. Rotate all of the jump rings to hide the cut ends.

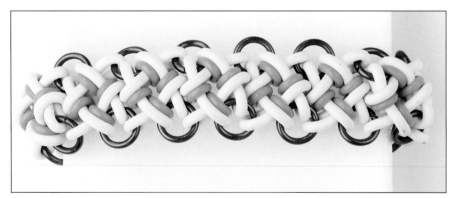

Notice how the square unit lies diagonally?
Try alternating two colors within each unit to emphasize this diagonal quality.

turbulent sea

You'll enjoy seeing this bracelet progress as it winds back
and forth like the rough ocean. A life preserver is optional.

materials + tools

24 light blue O-rings,
15 x 10 x 2.5 mm

48 dark green O-rings, 7 x 3 x 2 mm

24 turquoise O-rings, 12 x 8 x 2 mm

24 black O-rings, 7 x 3 x 2 mm

24 green 16-gauge anodized
aluminum jump rings, ³⁄₁₆ inch

Round-nose pliers

Flat-nose pliers, 2 pair

BASIC ELEMENT #1

instructions

1 Create 24 basic elements, each with one 15-mm O-ring and two dark green 7-mm O-rings (page 21). Create 24 additional basic elements, each with one 12-mm O-ring and one black 7-mm O-ring. Use the round-nose pliers to make all of the elements.

2 Insert the round-nose pliers through the end of one of the 15-mm elements, and pull one end of a 12-mm element through.

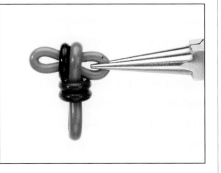

3 Open a jump ring using both flat-nose pliers for this process and as needed for the following steps (page 16). Lace the jump ring through the end of the 12-mm element you just pulled through.

4 insert the round-nose pliers through the end of a second 15-mm element, and pull through the free end of the 12-mm element you attached in step 2.

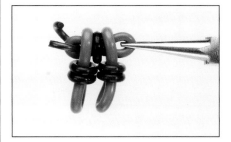

5 Open another jump ring. Lace it through the free end of the 12-mm element.

6 Insert the round-nose pliers, from the inside of the developing length, through the free end of the second 15-mm element. Pull another 12-mm element through.

7 Open a jump ring. Lace it through the end of the 12-mm element you just pulled through.

8 Insert the round-nose pliers through the end of a new 15-mm element, and pull the free end of the previously added 12-mm element through it.

9 Open a jump ring. Lace it through the free end of the 12-mm element you just pulled through.

10 Rotate the work. Insert the round-nose pliers, from the inside of the developing length, through the free end of the most recently added 15-mm element. Pull one end of another 12-mm element through.

11 Lace the closest open jump ring (to your left) through the closest end of the 12-mm element you just added. Close the jump ring.

12 Attach additional elements in the same manner until all are joined or the bracelet is the desired length.

13 Position the length so the beginning is on your left and the end is on your right. Insert the round-nose pliers through the

free end of the 15-mm element at the beginning of the length, from the inside of the developing piece. Grasp the free end of the 12-mm element at the end of the length. Pull it through.

14 Lace the closest open jump ring (to your left) through the free end of the 12-mm element you just pulled through. Close the jump ring.

15 Lace the last open jump ring at the beginning of the length, which is already attached, through the last free end at the end of the length, as shown in the photo. Close the jump ring. Rotate all of the jump rings to hide the cut ends.

oceana
BRACELET & EARRINGS

A basic element constructed around a heavy jump ring creates a
full-looking bracelet. The angular edges add an interesting touch.
Be sure to make the matching earrings.

bracelet instructions

1 Create one basic element using two 12-mm O-rings, one 7-mm O-ring, and two 3/16-inch jump rings laced on a closed 3/8-inch jump ring (page 22). Use both flat-nose pliers for this process and as needed for the following steps.

2 Open a 3/16-inch jump ring. Lace a third 12-mm O-ring through the same 3/8-inch jump ring used in step 1, placing it to the right of the two 12-mm O-rings.

3 Lace the open 3/16-inch jump ring through the ends in the third O-ring, and add a 7-mm O-ring. Close the jump ring. Open another 3/16-inch jump ring. Lace it through the central 12-mm O-ring.

4 Lace the same open jump ring through the 7-mm O-ring to the right. Close the jump ring.

5 Make a matching arrangement of elements on the opposite side of the same 3/8-inch jump ring. This is one unit.

6 Make nine additional units.

7 All of the finished units are rectangular, as shown in the photo. Reshape each unit into a square by tugging and pushing the edges with your fingers so it resembles the unit on the far right.

8 Lay all of the square units side by side on a flat surface. Arrange each one so a group of three attached elements is at the top and another group of three is at the bottom, as shown in the photo above.

bracelet materials + tools

60 blue O-rings, 12 x 8 x 2 mm

40 turquoise O-rings, 7 x 3 x 2 mm

120 turquoise 16-gauge anodized aluminum jump rings, 3/16 inch

10 turquoise 14-gauge anodized aluminum jump rings, 3/8 inch

Flat-nose pliers, 2 pair

BASIC ELEMENT #2

9 Open another 3/16-inch jump ring. Lace it through the 7-mm O-rings at the top corners of two neighboring units. Close the jump ring. Attach the neighboring bottom corners in the same units with another 3/16-inch jump ring.

10 Attach additional units in the same manner until you've joined them all or until the bracelet is the desired length.

11 Place the joined units on a flat surface so they're all side by side. Shift the first unit so it's above the others.

12 Open another ⅜-inch jump ring. Between the first and second units, lace the jump ring through the 7-mm O-ring that's shared by three closed ⅜-inch jump rings. Lace the same jump ring through the ends of the 12-mm O-ring that's shared by one closed ⅜-inch jump ring, as shown in the photo. Close the jump ring.

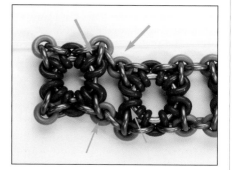

13 Attach the bottom corners between the first two units in the same manner, using another ⅜-inch jump ring.

14 Add an additional jump ring to each of the matched corners in the same manner.

Here's a bit of flash and fun: the double circles in each earring move independently of one another.

15 Join the beginning of the length to the end in the same manner. Rotate all of the jump rings to hide the cut ends.

earrings **instructions**

1 Create one basic element using two 12-mm O-rings, one 7-mm O-ring, and two ⅜-inch jump rings on a closed ⅜-inch jump ring (page 22).

2 Make another basic element on the same closed ⅜-inch jump ring.

3 Open two more ³⁄₁₆-inch jump rings. Lace one through each of the two center 12-mm O-rings. Close both jump rings.

4 Open another ³⁄₈-inch jump ring. Lace it through the two closed ³⁄₁₆-inch jump rings. Close the jump ring. This is the upper portion of the dangle.

5 Make two basic elements using four 12-mm O-rings, two 7-mm O-rings, and four ³⁄₁₆-inch jump rings on the empty ³⁄₈-inch jump ring you attached in step 4. Open two more ³⁄₁₆-inch jump rings. Lace one through each of the two center 12-mm O-rings and a 7-mm O-ring. Close both jump rings.

6 Open a ³⁄₁₆-inch jump ring. Lace it through the ³⁄₈-inch jump ring at the top of the earring. Close the jump ring. Open a ⁵⁄₃₂-inch jump ring. Lace it through the ³⁄₁₆-inch jump ring and the ear wire. Close the jump ring, and rotate all of the jump rings to hide the cut ends.

7 Repeat these instructions to make a matching earring.

earrings
materials + tools

16 blue O-rings, 12 x 8 x 2 mm

10 turquoise O-rings, 7 x 3 x 2 mm

26 turquoise 16-gauge anodized aluminum jump rings, ³⁄₁₆ inch

4 turquoise 14-gauge anodized aluminum jump rings, ³⁄₈ inch

2 turquoise 16-gauge anodized aluminum jump rings, ⁵⁄₃₂ inch

2 silver-plated kidney ear wires with loop and bead

Flat-nose pliers, 2 pair

BASIC ELEMENT #2

focal star
BRACELET

Showcase an outstanding handmade bead with an understated weave. The red jump rings along the edges echo a color in the bead.

instructions

1 Create 48 basic elements, each with one 15-mm O-ring and one 7-mm O-ring, using the round-nose pliers (page 21).

2 Insert the round-nose pliers through the end of one of the elements, and pull one end of a second element through the end of the first.

3 Insert the round-nose pliers through the other end of the first element. Pull one end of a third element through the end of the first. This is one unit.

4 Create 15 additional units.

5 Open a silver jump ring using both flat-nose pliers for this process and as needed for the following steps (page 16). Lace the jump ring through the two ends of the elements that come together at the point of a unit, as shown in the photo.

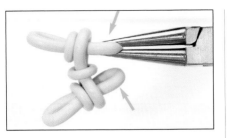

6 Lace the same open jump ring through the same two ends of a second unit. Close the jump ring. This jump ring is the center of the bracelet.

7 Open another silver jump ring. Lace it through the two ends that come together at a point in a third unit and through the center 7-mm O-ring of the second unit. Close the jump ring.

8 Open a red jump ring. Lace it into the third unit, through the neighboring 7-mm O-ring and the

materials + tools

48 white O-rings, 15 x 10 x 2.5 mm

48 white O-rings, 7 x 3 x 2 mm

2 white O-rings, 12 x 8 x 2 mm

15 silver-color 16-gauge etched aluminum jump rings, 3/16 inch

28 red 16-gauge anodized jump rings, 3/16 inch

12-inch (30.5 cm) length of 2-ply waxed linen string

Focal bead, 27 x 9 mm, with a hole large enough to hold a flattened 12-mm O-ring

Round-nose pliers

Flat-nose pliers, 2 pair

BASIC ELEMENT #1

FOCAL BEAD BY LISA WALSH

end of a 12-mm O-ring. Lace the same open jump ring through the end of an element in the second unit.

9 Open another red jump ring. Use it to join the remaining portions of the same two units as described in step 8.

10 Join another unit in the same manner, but positioning it on the opposite side of the center O-ring.

11 Add an equal number of additional units on both ends until you've joined all the units or until the bracelet is the desired length. When attaching the final unit on each end, lace the two outside edge jump rings but leave them open. You'll close these four jump rings later.

12 Insert the round-nose pliers through the free end of an O-ring in an outer element at one end of the bracelet. At the opposite end of the bracelet, pull the free end of an O-ring in the corresponding element through the end of the O-ring.

13 Join the beginning of the bracelet to the end at the bottom, in the same manner.

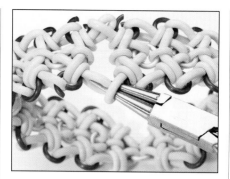

14 There are two free ends. Lace them through the nearest open jump rings. Close these two jump rings. Lace each of the two remaining open jump rings through the closest end of a 12-mm O-ring that doesn't have a jump ring yet, as shown in the photo.

15 Pull one of the 12-mm O-rings through the focal bead until enough of the O-ring is sticking out of the top for you to feel it when you run your fingers across the top of the bead. (See step 10 of Bright Blossom Necklace on page 92 for a photo of this process.) Lace the waxed linen string through the O-ring on the back of the bead and pull it through the top, center jump ring on the bracelet, from front to back. Pull both ends of the string through the jump ring.

16 Stop when the bottom of the focal bead rests on the top of the bracelet. Remove the string. Arrange the 12-mm O-ring with your fingers so the O-ring rests in the center of the jump ring. This centers the focal bead.

17 Lace the same string through the remaining 12-mm O-ring, and match up the ends. Pull this O-ring through the end of the 12-mm O-ring that's laced through the jump ring at the back of the focal bead. Using the round-nose pliers, center this O-ring and re-move the string. Rotate all of the jump rings to hide the cut ends.

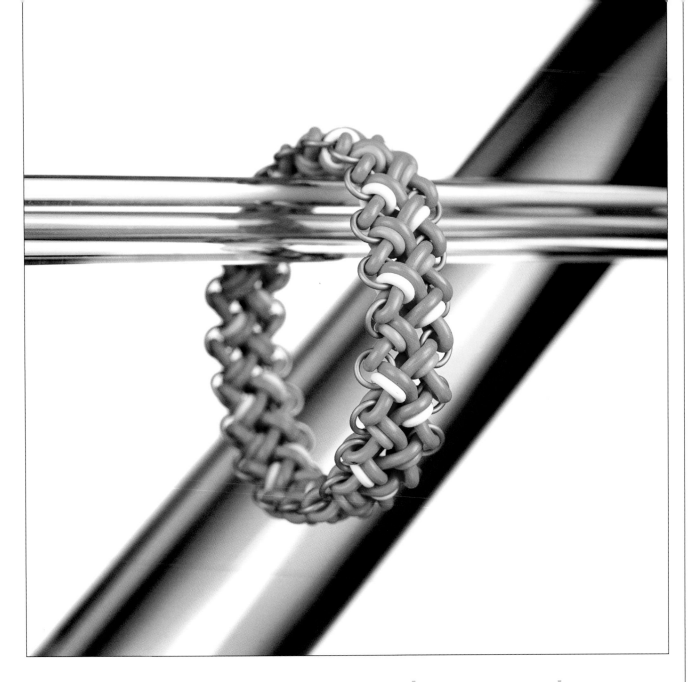

shades
OF AUTUMN

Lacing O-rings through other O-rings yields a
woven effect. To secure the ends, all you need to
do is close the linking jump rings.

materials + tools

44 orange O-rings, 15 x 10 x 2 mm

22 white O-rings, 7 x 3 x 2 mm

22 yellow O-rings, 7 x 3 x 2 mm

44 yellow 18-gauge anodized aluminum jump rings, ³⁄₁₆ inch

Round-nose pliers

Flat-nose pliers, 2 pair

BASIC ELEMENT #1

instructions

1 Using the round-nose pliers, create 22 basic elements, each with one 15-mm O-ring and one white 7-mm O-ring (page 21). Construct 22 additional elements using the remaining 15-mm O-rings and the yellow 7-mm O-rings.

2 Insert the round-nose pliers through the end of one of the elements with a white O-ring, and pull the end of a second element (one with a white O-ring) through the first.

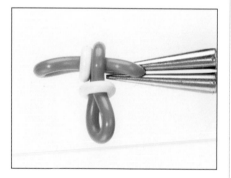

3 Flip the joined elements (A and B), and insert the round-nose pliers through a free end of Element B, on the side farthest from the 7-mm O-ring. Pull the end of a new element with a yellow O-ring (C) through.

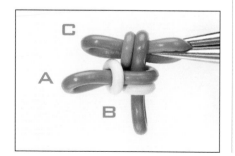

4 Add a fourth element that has a yellow O-ring (D).

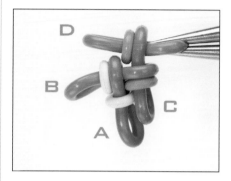

5 Open a jump ring, using both flat-nose pliers for this and other steps as needed (page 16). Lace the jump ring through the attached end of Element A and the 7-mm O-ring of the Element B.

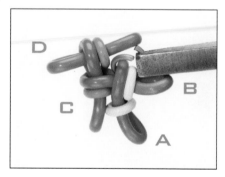

6 Lace the same open jump ring through the closest free end of the fourth element. Close the jump ring.

7 Add two more elements that have white O-rings (E and F) in the same manner.

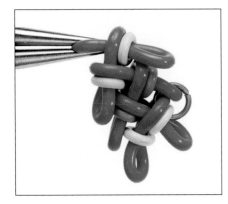

8 Open another jump ring and lace it through the attached end of Element B, 7-mm O-ring of Element C, and free end of Element E. Close the jump ring.

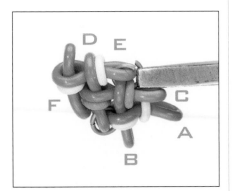

9 Add elements—two at a time and alternating the colors—in the same manner, each time using an open jump ring to lace the free end of the first new element to the closest 7-mm O-ring and the attached end of another element. Stop when you've joined all of the units or when the bracelet is the desired length.

10 Hold the length in your hand, with the beginning on your left and the end on the right. Remove the 7-mm O-ring on element A, as shown in the photo. Set it aside until step 12.

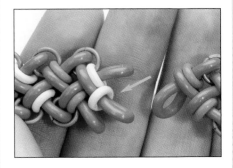

11 Insert the round-nose pliers though the end of the last attached element. Pull the free end of the first element through.

12 Release the element. Place the 7-mm O-ring over the end of the pliers, and grasp the free end of the first element in the pliers. Pull the O-ring off the pliers and onto the element.

13 Attach the last three jump rings in the same manner as in the previous steps.

bellflowers

A bit of weight added to an earring lets it move gracefully with the slightest turn of your head. These earrings showcase a vintage flower or drop bead.

instructions

1 Create three basic elements, each with one turquoise 12-mm O-ring, two yellow 4.8-mm O-rings, and one blue 4.8-mm O-ring, using the round-nose pliers (page 21).

2 Open one of the jump rings with both flat-nose pliers (page 16). Lace the jump ring through two of the basic elements. Close the jump ring, again using both flat-nose pliers (page 18).

3 Insert the round-nose pliers through the free end of one of the 12-mm O-rings. Pull the free end of a third element through the O-ring.

4 Insert the round-nose pliers through the end of the O-ring in the second (attached) element from step 2. Pull the free end of the third element through the second element.

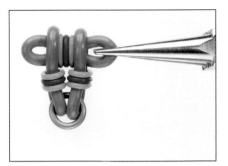

5 Open another jump ring. Lace it through the closed jump ring. Add the ear wire, and close the jump ring.

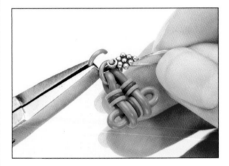

6 Glue the top of the acrylic flower inside the bead cap. Let the glue dry. Open another jump ring. Lace it through the loop at the top of the bead cap and then one of the free ends in the third element. Close the jump ring.

7 Attach the acrylic flower/bead cap to the last free end in the third element. Rotate all of the jump rings to hide the cut ends.

8 Repeat these instructions to make the matching earring.

materials + tools

6 turquoise O-rings, 12 x 8 x 2 mm

12 yellow O-rings, 4.8 x 8 x 1 mm

6 blue O-rings, 4.8 x 8 x 1 mm

8 yellow 18-gauge anodized aluminum jump rings, 3/16-inch

4 bead caps with loop, 7 x 7 mm

Strong-bonding glue that dries clear

4 vintage acrylic flowers, 7 x 12 mm

2 silver-plated kidney ear wires with loop and bead

Round-nose pliers

Flat-nose pliers, 2 pair

BASIC ELEMENT #1

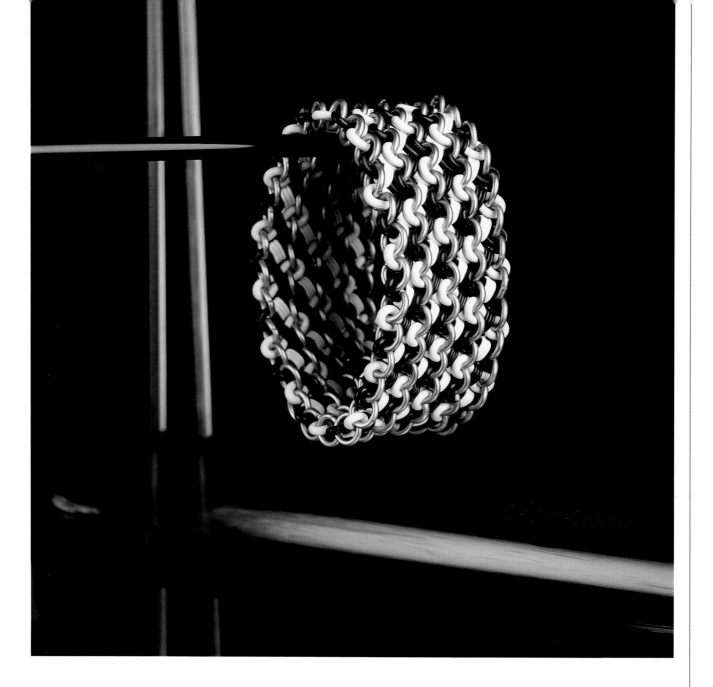

woven cuff

There's no denying the beauty of this bracelet. It's
the widest band in this book and will look
spectacular on your wrist.

instructions

1 Use the round-nose pliers to create 56 basic elements, each from one white 12-mm O-ring and three dark green 4.8-mm O-rings (page 21). Then create 56 more basic elements, each from one dark green 12-mm O-ring and three white 4.8-mm O-rings.

2 Open a jump ring, using both flat-nose pliers (page 16). Lace the jump ring through one end of two dark green, and then two white elements. Close the jump ring, again using both flat-nose pliers.

3 Rotate the un-attached ends of the elements next to each other as shown in the photo.

4 Open another jump ring. Lace it through the free ends of the two bottom elements. Close the jump ring.

5 Open another jump ring. Rotate the joined elements, and lace the open jump ring through the free ends of the two elements at the top. Lace another white element and another dark green element onto the jump ring to match the orientation of the joined elements. Close the jump ring.

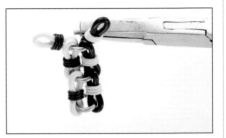

6 Repeat step 5.

7 Open another jump ring. Lace it through the free ends of the top two elements. Close the jump ring.

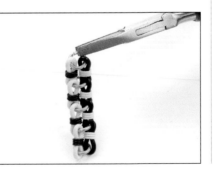

materials + tools

56 dark green O-rings, 12 x 8 x 2 mm

56 white O-rings, 12 x 8 x 2 mm

168 dark green O-rings, 4.8 x 2.8 x 1 mm

168 white O-rings, 4.8 x 2.8 x 1 mm

140 gold 16-gauge anodized aluminum jump rings, ³⁄₁₆ inch

Round-nose pliers

Flat-nose pliers, 2 pair

BASIC ELEMENT #1

8 Open another jump ring. Lace it through the overlapping ends of the white elements at the top right side of the developing piece.

9 Lace two dark green elements onto the same jump ring. Straighten out the new elements so they sit against their white neighbors. Close the jump ring.

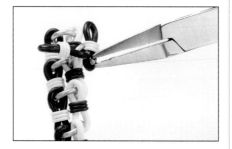

10 Open another jump ring. Lace it through the top end of the joined white element and through the free end of the dark green element you just added. Close the jump ring. Attach all the jump rings on the same side of the jump ring they're next to.

11 Open another jump ring. Lace it through the ends of the next available overlapping elements and the free end of the remaining dark green element. Lace another dark green element onto the open jump ring. Close the jump ring.

12 Repeat step 11. Open another jump ring. Use it to attach the remaining loose element to the one beside it. Close the jump ring. This is the third vertical row and represents the width of the bracelet.

13 Repeat steps 8 to 12, lacing on columns of alternating colors until all of the elements are joined or until the bracelet is the desired length. Make sure you end with a column that's the opposite color than the very first column.

14 Force all of the attached elements to make diagonal lines.

15 To join the columns and form the bracelet, start by opening another jump ring. Beginning in the center of the first and last columns, lace the opened jump ring through two sets of aligning elements (one should be white, the other dark green). You are lacing through one set, just as all the other columns are joined. Close the jump ring.

16 One at a time, join the next two elements in the same manner. Open a jump ring, lace it through the neighboring elements, and close each jump ring in turn.

17 At the top and bottom of the columns you're joining, lace the remaining two jump rings through the very end O-rings on each side. Rotate all of the jump rings so the cut ends are on the underside of the bracelet.

golden crosses

Four elements, many combinations. If you loved the square units in Rays of Sunshine (page 48), you'll enjoy this project as well.

materials + tools

40 rust O-rings, 7 x 3 x 2 mm

40 yellow O-rings, 12 x 8 x 2 mm

40 dark green O-rings,
15 x 10 x 2.5 mm

20 yellow 18-gauge anodized
aluminum jump rings, ³⁄₁₆ inch

Round-nose pliers

Flat-nose pliers, 2 pair

BASIC ELEMENT #3

instructions

1 Make a basic element, starting with a 7-mm O-ring centered on a 12-mm O-ring. Then add a 15-mm O-ring to complete the element (page 24). Create 39 additional basic elements in the same manner, always using the round-nose pliers.

2 Insert the round-nose pliers through the end of one of the elements, and pull the end of a second element through. Position the 7-mm O-rings to the outside.

3 Insert the round-nose pliers through the opposite end of the second element, and pull the end of a third element through, again with the 7-mm O-ring to the outside.

4 Insert the round-nose pliers through the opposite end of the third element, and pull the end of a fourth element through with the 7-mm O-ring to the outside.

5 Insert the round-nose pliers through the opposite end of the fourth element, and pull the free end of the first element through. This is one unit.

6 Create nine additional units.

7 Shift every wrapped yellow and rust basic element in every unit so each one sits up against the next overlapping element. Lay all the units side by side on a flat surface, all oriented in the same manner.

8 Open one of the jump rings using both flat-nose pliers (page 16). Lace it through the end of an O-ring in one of the units.

9 Lace the same open jump ring through the ends of two O-rings in a second unit. Close the jump ring, again using both flat-nose pliers.

10 Join the bottoms of the same units in the same manner.

11 Attach additional units by joining the top and bottom of each one in the same manner until you've used all the units or until you reach the desired length for your bracelet.

12 Join the beginning of the bracelet to the end with two jump rings and the established process. Rotate all of the jump rings to hide the cut ends.

playful heart

All eyes will focus on the outstanding handmade
bead showcased on this long necklace. Choose a
simple color combination for an understated chain.

instructions

1 Close two of the silver ⅜-inch jump rings. Open two of the ³⁄₁₆-inch jump rings, and lace both of them through the two closed jump rings. Close the jump rings. Use both of the flat-nose pliers to open and close the jump rings (pages 16 to 18).

2 Create one basic element using two 12-mm O-rings, one 7-mm O-ring, and two ³⁄₁₆-inch jump rings on one attached, closed ⅜-inch jump ring (page 22).

3 Attach another basic element of the same color to the remaining attached, closed ⅜-inch jump ring.

4 Open a silver ⅜-inch jump ring. Lace it through the two ³⁄₁₆-inch jump rings in one of the elements. Position this jump ring so it's on top

of the 7-mm O-ring. Close the jump ring. This is the underside of the necklace.

5 Add length to both sides of the developing necklace by attaching basic elements and silver jump rings in the same manner until there are a total of 21 basic elements on each side. Add two more elements to each side, this time using the bronze ⅜-inch jump rings. At both ends, finish by adding the remaining bronze jump rings.

6 Open a ½-inch jump ring. Lace it through the last ³⁄₁₆-inch jump ring at each end. Close the jump ring.

materials + tools

92 yellow O-rings, 12 x 8 x 2 mm

46 turquoise O-rings, 7 x 3 x 2 mm

42 silver-color 14-gauge etched aluminum jump rings, ⅜ inch

94 green 16-gauge anodized aluminum jump rings, ³⁄₁₆ inch

4 bronze-color 14-gauge anodized jump rings, ⅜ inch

Gold-color 14-gauge anodized aluminum jump ring, ½ inch

Black 14-gauge anodized aluminum jump ring, ⅜ inch

Focal bead with top drill, 28 x 29 mm, with a hole large enough to fit a ⅜-inch jump ring

Flat-nose pliers, 2 pair

BASIC ELEMENT #2

FOCAL BEAD BY STEPHANIE SERSICH

7 Open the black jump ring. Lace it through the bead and the ½-inch jump ring. Close the jump ring. Rotate all of the jump rings to hide the cut ends.

black & white

Black and white—especially when woven together—create

a stunning combination. You won't be able to take

your eyes off this mesmerizing pattern.

instructions

1   Refer to page 21 to learn how to make a variation on the basic element with several small O-rings—instead of just one—situated on a larger O-ring. Make units in various combinations of white and black according to the chart on this page. All the units have three small O-rings (two of one color and a single in the other color) mounted on a larger O-ring. In every case, when you place the small O-rings on the pliers, always add the single-color O-ring second, in between the other two.

2   Insert the round-nose pliers through the end of one Unit A. Pull a Unit B through it. Insert the pliers through the opposite end of the first unit, and pull another Unit B through.

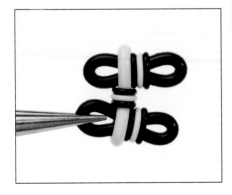

3   Insert the pliers through one end of another Unit A, and pull the second unit through it. Insert the pliers through the opposite end of the fourth unit (the second Unit A), and pull the third element (the second Unit B) through it. This is one square foundation piece. I call it a white square in the following steps because the white 12-mm O-rings overlap the black.

4   Create six additional white squares.

5   Create seven black squares. Start with a Unit C in the first position, and then add a Unit D second, a Unit C third, and a Unit D fourth.

6   Lay out all the squares on a flat surface, starting with a white one and alternating black and white thereafter.

	Number of Units	12-mm O-Ring Color	4.8-mm O-Ring Colors
Unit A	28	white	two black, one white
Unit B	14	black	two black, one white
Unit C	28	black	two white, one black
Unit D	14	white	two white, one black

42 black O-rings, 12 x 8 x 2 mm

42 white O-rings, 12 x 8 x 2 mm

84 black O-rings, 4.8 x 2.8 x 1 mm

84 white O-rings, 4.8 x 2.8 x 1 mm

28 black 18-gauge anodized aluminum jump rings, ³⁄₁₆ inch

Round-nose pliers

Flat-nose pliers, 2 pair

BASIC ELEMENT #1

7 Open a jump ring using both flat-nose pliers (page 16). Lace the jump ring through one end of another Unit C. Lace the same jump ring through two neighboring free ends of a white square and then one end of another Unit A. Close the jump ring, again with both flat-nose pliers.

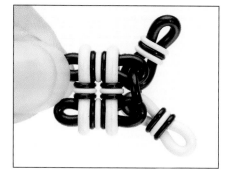

8 Add another two units to the bottom of the same white square, this time placing a Unit A on the jump ring before lacing it through the free ends of the white square. Finish by adding a Unit C last, as shown in the photo. This photo shows the underside of the square. When right side up (when resting on a flat surface), the four added units sit on top of the square.

9 Place a Unit A and a Unit C between each white and black square already on the flat surface.

10 Open another jump ring. With the attached units and squares face-down, lace the jump ring through a free end of a second (black) square, one end of another Unit C, one end of another Unit A, and the neighboring free end of the same black square.

11 Repeat step 10 to join the remaining free end of the black square.

12 Attach additional units and squares to both sides of the joined ones in the same manner until you have joined all but one of the squares. Continue to alternate the colors of the units and the squares.

13 Turn the length right side up. Open a jump ring. Lace it through two of the free ends of the loose square you set aside in step 12. Lace the same jump ring

through the end of a loose unit already attached at each end of the joined squares. Close the jump ring. Join the beginning of the length to the end at the remaining loose corner in the same manner. Rotate all of the jump rings to hide the cut ends.

it's a guy
THING

Contrasting colors and shapes work together to form a perfect band with beautiful straight edges. Choose O-rings in a friend's favorite colors and make one as a gift.

materials + tools

44 white O-rings, 15 x 10 x 2.5 mm

22 black O-rings, 7 x 3 x 2 mm

22 brick red O-rings, 7 x 3 x 2 mm

44 blue O-rings, 9 x 5 x 2 mm

44 silver-color 16-gauge etched
aluminum jump rings, ³⁄₁₆ inch

Round-nose pliers

Flat-nose pliers, 2 pair

BASIC ELEMENT #1

instructions

1 Using the round-nose pliers, create 44 basic elements, each with one 15-mm O-ring and one 7-mm O-ring (page 21). Make half of the elements with the black 7-mm O-rings and use the brick red 7-mm O-rings to make the remaining elements.

2 Insert the round-nose pliers through one end of a brick red and white element, and pull one end of a white and black element through.

3 Rotate the joined elements, and insert the round-nose pliers through the free end of the second element. Pull the free end of the first element through.

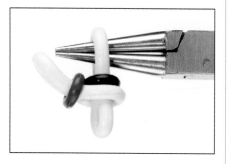

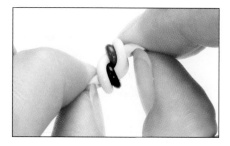

4 Grab each of the two free ends with the thumb and forefinger of your hands and pull the ends diagonally. This is one unit.

5 Create 21 additional units.

6 Lay one unit on a flat surface so the top of the unit has an element with a black O-ring overlapping the element with a brick red O-ring. Lay a second unit on the flat surface, this time rotating the unit so the top has an element with a brick red O-ring overlapping the element with a black O-ring.

7 Lay the rest of the units on a flat surface, rotating every other unit to repeat the orientation established by the first two.

8 Open a jump ring using both flat-nose pliers (page 16). Lace the jump ring through the attached, overlapped end of an element at the top of the first unit and the free end of the element at the top of the second unit.

9 Lace the same open jump ring through two of the 9-mm O-rings. Close the jump ring, again using both flat-nose pliers (page 18).

10 Rotate the joined units and repeat steps 8 and 9 with another jump ring and two 9-mm O-rings.

11 Attach additional units until you've joined all of them or until the bracelet is the desired length.

12 Open two jump rings. Lace them through the two previously added 9-mm O-rings, the unit previously attached, and then a new unit. Lace on two more 9-mm O-rings, and close the jump rings.

13 Join the beginning to the end of the length with two jump rings in the same way you attached the previous units. Rotate all of the jump rings to hide the cut ends.

shades of jade
NECKLACE & EARRINGS

Mix it up with square acrylic beads that contrast the round O-rings and jump rings. These eye-catching focal units create a festive aspect for the necklace. The matching earrings complete the ensemble.

necklace **instructions**

1 Make a basic element using the round-nose pliers. Start with a 7-mm O-ring centered on a turquoise 12-mm O-ring, and then add a blue 12-mm O-ring (page 24). Create 17 additional basic elements in the same manner.

2 Open one of the ⅜-inch jump rings, and lace it through a free end of one of the elements. Use both flat-nose pliers for this process and as needed for the following steps (page 16).

3 Lace the same open jump ring through the other free end of the same element.

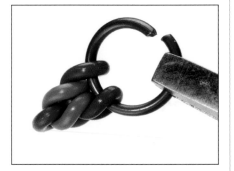

4 Lace both ends of two more elements onto the same open jump ring to complete the first focal unit.

5 Make five more focal units in the same manner. Set these aside.

6 Open a ¼-inch jump ring, and lace it through an acrylic square. Close the jump ring. Open two ¼-inch jump rings, and lace both of them through the jump ring you just closed. Lace the same open jump rings through one of the acrylic rings. Close the jump rings.

7 Open two more ¼-inch jump rings, and lace them through the same acrylic ring and another ¼-inch jump ring. Close the open jump rings, and open the single jump ring you just added. Lace it through another acrylic square and then close it. This is the necklace's center chain unit.

necklace
materials + tools

18 brick red O-rings, 7 x 3 x 2 mm

18 turquoise O-rings, 12 x 8 x 2 mm

18 blue O-rings, 12 x 8 x 2 mm

6 violet 16-gauge anodized aluminum jump rings, ⅜ inch

84 turquoise 16-gauge anodized aluminum jump rings, ¼ inch

2 turquoise 16-gauge anodized aluminum jump rings, ³⁄₁₆ inch

12 light green acrylic square beads, 11 x 11 mm, with holes large enough to fit two ¼-inch jump rings

13 purple acrylic rings, 11 mm OD (page 11), with holes large enough to fit four ¼-inch jump rings

Antique gold toggle clasp, 17 mm

Round-nose pliers

Flat-nose pliers, 2 pair

BASIC ELEMENT #3

8 Open a ¼-inch jump ring, and lace it through one of the acrylic squares in the center chain unit. Attach two ¼-inch jump rings, another acrylic ring, two more ¼-inch jump rings, a single ¼-inch jump ring, and another acrylic square.

9 Repeat step 8 two more times to build the necklace's length at one side, then repeat it three times to add length to the opposite side of the center chain unit. You should now have eight acrylic squares on a length.

10 Open the jump ring in one of the focal units, and lace it through the single jump ring on both sides of an acrylic square in the center of the length. Close the jump ring. Open a ¼-inch jump ring, and lace it through the pair of jump rings on each side of the same acrylic square.

11 Add focal units and ¼-inch jump rings to the remaining five acrylic squares at the center of the length.

12 Add length to one end of the chain unit in the established order, without acrylic squares, as follows: one ¼-inch jump ring, a pair of ¼-inch jump rings, one acrylic ring, a pair of ¼-inch jump rings, one ¼-inch jump ring. Close all the jump rings as you attach them. Add the

same items—in the same order—to the other end of the necklace. Repeat this process at both ends until all of the items are attached or the necklace is the desired length, beginning with an acrylic square.

13 Open the two ³⁄₁₆-inch jump rings. Lace one of them through the loop on the toggle bar and the last item at one end of the chain. Lace the second jump ring through the toggle ring and the other end of the chain. Close both jump rings.

The set will look stunning with attire that enhances the colors and shapes.

earrings instructions

1 Follow steps 1 to 4 of the necklace instructions (page 81) to make three basic elements (page 24) on one of the ⅜-inch jump rings. This is one focal unit.

2 Open one of the ³⁄₁₆-inch jump rings and lace it through a closed ³⁄₁₆-inch jump ring. Close the jump ring. Make another chain in the same manner.

3 Open two ¼-inch jump rings, and lace them through the acrylic square, the focal unit's jump ring, and a jump ring in one of the chains. Close the jump ring. Use another ¼-inch jump ring to attach

 the second chain and the same acrylic square and focal unit.

4 Open a ³⁄₁₆-inch jump ring. Lace this jump ring through the two ³⁄₁₆-inch jump rings attached to the ¼-inch jump rings. It will be horizontal. Close these two jump rings.

5 Open a ³⁄₁₆-inch jump ring. Lace it through the uppermost, ³⁄₁₆-inch jump ring at the top of each attached chain. Lace the same jump ring through the earring loop. Close the jump ring.

6 Repeat these instructions to make the matching earring.

6 brick red O-rings, 7 x 3 x 2 mm

6 blue O-rings, 12 x 8 x 2 mm

6 turquoise O-rings, 12 x 8 x 2 mm

2 turquoise 16-gauge anodized aluminum jump rings, ⅜ inch

12 turquoise 16-gauge anodized aluminum jump rings, ³⁄₁₆ inch

4 turquoise 16-gauge anodized aluminum jump rings, ¼ inch

2 light green acrylic square beads, 9 mm, with holes large enough for two ¼-inch jump rings

2 sterling silver kidney ear wires with loop and bead, 10.4 x 18.6 mm

Round-nose pliers

Flat-nose pliers, 2 pair

BASIC ELEMENT #3

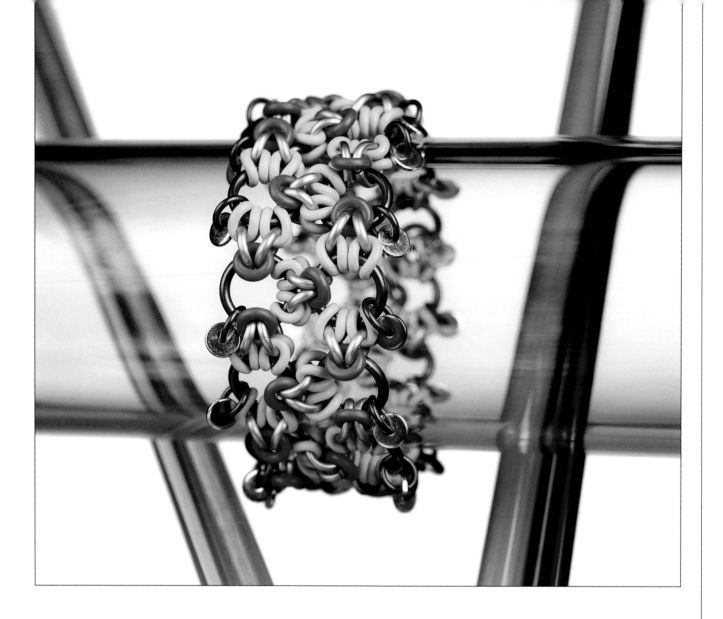

santa fe
AUTUMN

Small disks bring a new effect to a common technique for attaching beads to chain mail. When worn, the metal reflects light as you move.

instructions

1 Create one basic element using two 12-mm O-rings, one 7-mm O-ring, and two 16-gauge ³/₁₆-inch jump rings on a ³/₈-inch jump ring (page 22). Use the flat-nose pliers for this process and as needed for the following steps.

2 Open another ³/₈-inch jump ring. Lace it through the two 16-gauge ³/₁₆-inch jump rings in the basic element so the jump ring lies underneath the 7-mm O-ring. Close the jump ring.

3 Make another basic element on the recently added ³/₈-inch jump ring. Attach two 12-mm O-rings, one 7-mm O-ring, and two 16-gauge ³/₁₆-inch jump rings. Always place the jump ring underneath the 7-mm O-ring.

4 Add two more elements, repeating steps 2 and 3. Turn over the developing unit so the 7-mm O-rings are on top. This is the exterior of the bracelet.

5 Open the first ³/₈-inch jump ring. Lace it through the last two ³/₁₆-inch jump rings so it's underneath the 7-mm O-ring. Again, make sure the jump ring is positioned underneath the 7-mm O-ring.

6 Rotate the unit so the 7-mm O-rings are on top, as shown in the photo. Make a new basic element around the attached ³/₈-inch jump ring at the bottom right.

7 Open another ³/₈-inch jump ring. Lace it through the two ³/₁₆-inch jump rings you just attached (and underneath the 7-mm O-ring). Close the jump ring. Make another basic element around the ³/₈-inch jump ring you just attached.

materials + tools

72 yellow O-rings, 12 x 8 x 2 mm

36 rust O-rings, 7 x 3 x 2 mm

72 gold-color 16-gauge anodized aluminum jump rings, ³/₁₆ inch

24 bronze-color 14-gauge anodized aluminum jump rings, ³/₈ inch

24 gold-color 18-gauge anodized aluminum jump rings, ³/₁₆ inch

24 silver-color center-drilled, disk-shaped beads, 6 mm, with holes large enough to fit a ³/₁₆-inch, 18-gauge jump ring

Flat-nose pliers, 2 pair

BASIC ELEMENT #2

8 Open another ⅜-inch jump ring. Lace it through the two recently added ³⁄₁₆-inch jump rings (and underneath the 7-mm O-ring). Close the jump ring. Wrap a 12-mm O-ring around the jump ring you just closed. Open a 16-gauge ³⁄₁₆-inch jump ring, and lace it through the ends of the 12-mm O-ring and another 7-mm O-ring.

9 Lace the same open jump ring through the attached ⅜-inch jump ring above and to the left. Make sure the 7-mm O-ring is to the right side of the opened ³⁄₁₆-inch jump ring. Close the jump ring.

10 Attach a second 12-mm O-ring and opened ³⁄₁₆-inch jump ring to the most recently attached ⅜-inch jump ring, the ⅜-inch jump ring, and the 7-mm O-ring from step 9. This is one unit.

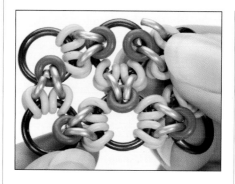

11 Repeat steps 6 to 8, this time starting the process by attaching the first items to the top right ⅜-inch jump ring.

12 Repeat steps 8 and 9, this time attaching the length to the bottom left ⅜-inch jump ring. You have completed a second unit.

13 Add eight additional units in the same manner. As you add the units, you'll see the 7-mm O-ring in the center switch sides every second element.

14 Hold the beginning of the length at the top and bring the end around to match at the bottom. Join the ends with a 12-mm O-ring, an opened 16-gauge ³⁄₁₆-inch jump ring, and lace a 7-mm O-ring on the jump ring. Close the jump ring. Re-

peat on the other side of the bracelet, switching directions.

15 Attach the last 12-mm O-ring and 16-gauge ³⁄₁₆-inch jump ring on both sides of the bracelet.

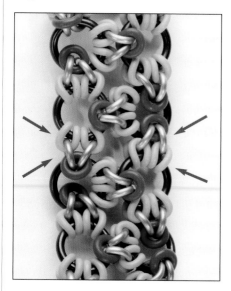

16 Open a 18-gauge ³⁄₁₆-inch jump ring. Lace it through one of the beads. Lace the same jump ring through a ⅜-inch jump ring. Close the jump ring. Add the remaining beads and jump rings to the bracelet in the same manner.

terra cotta
BAND

Wear a wide band for instant drama. The
interlocking rings create gentle curves
and swirls that dance around your wrist.

materials + tools

20 brick red O-rings, 15 x 10 x 2.5 mm

20 rust O-rings, 15 x 10 x 2.5 mm

40 black O-rings, 7 x 3 x 2 mm

40 black O-rings, 9 x 5 x 2 mm

30 gold-color 16-gauge anodized aluminum jump rings, ³⁄₁₆ inch

20 bronze-color 16-gauge anodized aluminum jump rings, ¼ inch

Round-nose pliers

Flat-nose pliers, 2 pair

BASIC ELEMENT #1

instructions

1 Use the round-nose pliers to create 40 basic elements, each with one 15-mm O-ring and one 7-mm O-ring (page 21). Half of the finished elements will have a brick red (Color A) O-ring; the others will have a rust (Color B) O-ring.

2 Open a ³⁄₁₆-inch jump ring using both of the flat-nose pliers for this process and as needed for the following steps (page 16). Lace the jump ring through the 7-mm O-rings of two of the elements, using one of each color.

3 Lace the same open jump ring through the 7-mm O-rings of two more elements, alternating the colors. Close the jump ring, forcing the elements close together to make room for the pliers to get a firm grip.

4 Arrange the elements in a square, with the shared jump ring in the center. Open a ³⁄₁₆-inch jump ring. Lace it through one of the 7-mm O-rings. Lace two 9-mm O-rings onto the open jump ring. Close the jump ring. Add another ³⁄₁₆-inch jump ring and two 9-mm O-rings to the element directly opposite in the same manner. This is one square unit.

5 Create nine additional units.

6 Open a ¼-inch jump ring. Using two neighboring elements, lace it through the 15-mm and 9-mm O-rings at one corner of both units. Close the jump ring.

7 Rotate the joined units. Open a ¼-inch jump ring. Lace it through the neighboring 15-mm and 9-mm O-rings of both units. Close the jump ring.

8 Attach additional units to the joined ones in the same manner until all of the units are joined or until the bracelet is the desired length.

9 Join the beginning of the length to the end with two ¼-inch jump rings the same way you attached the previous units. Rotate all of the jump rings to hide the cut ends.

Along with the curves and swirls here,
check out the rectangles created by the black O-rings.

bright blossom
NECKLACE

In this piece, woven units cascade into a free-form bead. Learn how to work this disk-like shape into a necklace using O-rings.

instructions

1 Create 40 of the basic elements, each with two turquoise 12-mm O-rings and one blue 7-mm O-ring, using the round-nose pliers (page 24). Construct eight more basic elements using two dark green 12-mm and one blue 7-mm O-ring.

2 Open one of the yellow ³⁄₁₆-inch jump rings using both flat-nose pliers (page 16). Lace the jump ring through a free end of a finished turquoise and blue element.

3 Lace the same jump ring through the opposite end of the same element with the blue 7-mm O-ring on the outside.

4 Lace the same jump ring through both free ends of another turquoise and blue element. This is one two-part unit.

5 Create 19 additional turquoise two-part units, and four dark green two-part units (also using the yellow ³⁄₁₆-inch jump rings).

6 Lace a 7-mm O-ring in a turquoise two-part unit onto the open jump ring in a second turquoise two-part unit. Close the same jump ring.

7 Rotate the joined units so the second unit is to your left. Lace the closest 7-mm O-ring in the second unit onto the open jump ring in the first unit. Close the jump ring. This is one linear unit.

8 Make nine additional turquoise and two dark green linear units.

9 Open a ⁵⁄₃₂-inch jump ring. Lace it through the 7-mm jump ring at the end of two turquoise linear units. Close the jump ring. Continue attaching linear units end to end, in

materials + tools

80 turquoise O-rings, 12 x 8 x 2 mm

48 blue O-rings, 7 x 3 x 2 mm

16 dark green O-rings, 12 x 8 x 2 mm

5 yellow O-rings, 12 x 8 x 2 mm

5 yellow O-rings, 7 x 3 x 2 mm

3 turquoise O-rings, 7 x 3 x 2 mm

24 yellow 18-gauge anodized aluminum jump rings, ³⁄₁₆ inch

16 yellow 18-gauge anodized aluminum jump rings, ⁵⁄₃₂ inch

2 orange 16-gauge anodized aluminum jump rings, ⁵⁄₁₆ inch

3 red 16-gauge anodized aluminum jump rings, ³⁄₁₆ inch

Turquoise 16-gauge anodized aluminum jump ring, ¼ inch

12-inch (30.5 cm) length of 2-ply waxed linen string

Focal bead, center-drilled, 29 x 31 mm, with a hole large enough to hold a flattened 12-mm O-ring

3 silver-color flower bead caps, 7 x 6 mm

Antique gold plated toggle clasp, 17 mm

Round-nose pliers

Flat-nose pliers, 2 pair

Sharp scissors

BASIC ELEMENT #3

FOCAL BEAD BY BRONWEN HEILMAN

the same manner, until the length has five turquoise linear units. Attach one dark green linear unit to the fifth turquoise unit. Make another necklace chain in the same manner. Set both aside.

10 Lace the waxed linen string through two 12-mm O-rings. Insert the ends through the focal bead from front to back. Holding the focal bead in your left hand, tightly grip the string with your right and pull. This stretches the two O-rings as they squeeze through the hole in the bead. Stop pulling when a third of both O-rings emerge from the back of the bead. Remove the string.

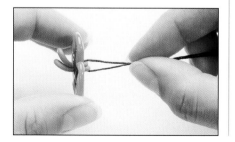

11 Snip the ends of the O-rings that are exposed on the front of the focal bead using the sharp scissors.

12 Open two ⁵⁄₁₆-inch jump rings. Lace them through the two O-ring loops protruding from the back of the bead. Lace one of the jump rings through the dark green end of both of the necklace chains. Close this jump ring.

13 Create a Basic Element #1 using one of the yellow 12-mm O-rings and a turquoise 7-mm O-ring (page 21). Open a red ³⁄₁₆-inch jump ring, and lace it through both ends of the element. Close the jump ring. Thread the waxed linen through the attached 7-mm O-ring, and pull the ends through one of the bead caps (until the bottom of the bead cap rests against the yellow 12-mm O-ring). Remove the string. This is one constructed dangle bead.

14 Make two more dangles beads in the same manner.

15 Lace two yellow 7-mm O-rings onto the open ⁵⁄₁₆-inch jump ring laced on the back of the focal bead. Close the jump ring. Open a ¼-inch jump ring, and lace it through the two 7-mm O-rings and the jump rings at the top of all three dangles. Close the jump ring.

16 Open six yellow ⁵⁄₃₂-inch jump rings. Attach a three-ring chain to the unattached ends of the chain. Open the third ring on one end of the chain, and lace it through the loop on the toggle bar. Close the jump ring. Repeat on the other chain and attach the toggle ring.

x's & o's

Create the universal symbol for hugs and kisses
with O-rings and jump rings. Give this sweet
bracelet to someone you love.

materials + tools

56 turquoise O-rings, 12 x 8 x 2 mm

28 black O-rings, 10 x 6 x 2 mm

14 violet 18-gauge anodized aluminum jump rings, ³⁄₁₆ inch

14 black 18-gauge anodized aluminum jump rings, ³⁄₁₆ inch

Round-nose pliers

Flat-nose pliers, 2 pair

BASIC ELEMENT #2

instructions

1 Create a variation on the basic element (page 22). Open two violet jump rings using both flat-nose pliers (page 16). Use your fingers to squeeze together two 12-mm O-rings and then insert them through one of the 10-mm O-rings. Lace a jump ring through both free ends of one of the 12-mm jump rings. Wrap and secure the second 12-mm O-ring in the same manner.

2 Create a basic element using one 12-mm O-ring and one 10-mm O-ring. Open a black jump ring, and lace it through the ends of the 12-mm O-ring.

3 Insert the round-nose pliers through the 10-mm O-ring in the first element. Grasp the free end of the element you created in step 2, and pull the 10-mm O-ring through the center of the first element.

4 Insert the round-nose pliers through the free end of the 10-mm O-ring you just pulled through. Pull the end of another 12-mm O-ring through the attached O-ring.

5 Open a black jump ring. Lace it through the free ends of the 12-mm O-ring. This is one unit.

6 Create a basic element using one 12-mm and one 10-mm O-ring. Lace the jump ring from step 5 through the free ends of the 12-mm O-ring in the first unit. Close the jump ring.

7 Wrap a 12-mm O-ring around the 10-mm O-ring at the end of the developing length. Lace a black jump ring through the ends of the 12-mm O-ring.

8 Make another basic element. Lace the open, attached violet jump ring at the bottom right of the unit through both free ends of the new element. Close the jump ring.

9 Insert the round-nose pliers through the 10-mm O-ring in the element added in step 6. Pull the 10-mm O-ring in the element added in step 8 through the other O-ring.

10 Insert the round-nose pliers through the 10-mm O-ring you just pulled through. Pull the end of another 12-mm O-ring through the 10-mm O-ring.

11 Open another violet jump ring. Lace it through the free ends of the 12-mm O-ring. This completes a second unit.

12 Add 11 additional units in the same manner, alternating violet and black jump rings along the edges.

13 Make another variation of the basic element using one 12-mm O-ring and one 10-mm O-ring and securing the free ends by lacing it with the open jump ring at the bottom of the first unit at the beginning of the length. Close the jump ring. Wrap a second 12-mm O-ring around the same 10-mm O-ring. Lace the last previously attached jump ring through both ends of the 12-mm O-ring. Close the jump ring.

14 Make a basic element and attach it to the top right jump ring at the beginning of the length. Close the jump ring.

15 Insert the round-nose pliers through the 10-mm O-ring you added in step 13. Pull the free end of the 10-mm O-ring you just added through the O-ring.

16 Secure the end you just pulled through by inserting a 12-mm O-ring through it.

17 Lace the remaining open jump ring through the free ends of the 12-mm O-ring you just added. Close the jump ring. Rotate all of the jump rings to hide the cut ends.

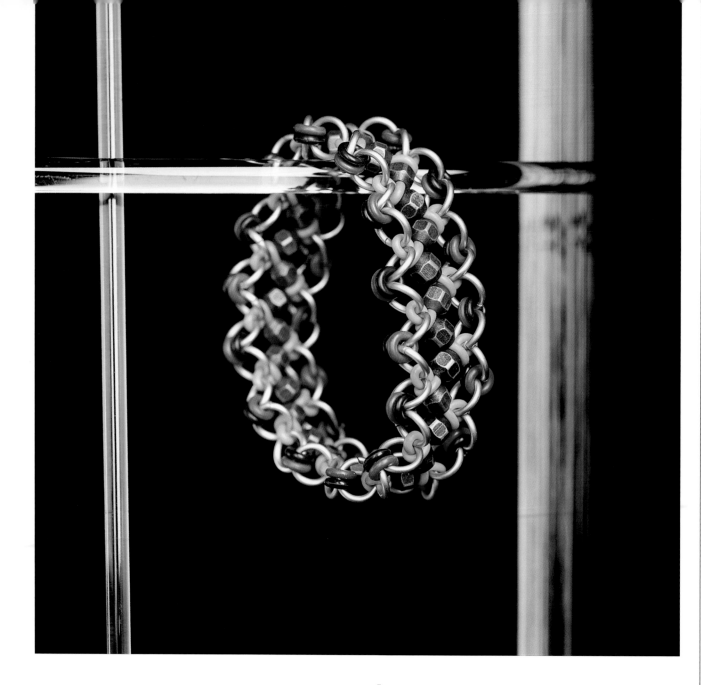

etruscan
GOLD

This weighty, creative bracelet looks and feels expensive.

You'll love using the bead in place of the O-ring.

instructions

1 Lace the waxed linen string through one of the 12-mm O-rings, and line up the two ends. Insert the ends through the bead, and pull on them until the O-ring is squeezed through the bead. Stop when the bead is centered on the O-ring. Remove the string. Create 25 additional basic elements in the same manner.

2 Insert the round-nose pliers through one end of the first element (A) and pull the end of a second element (B) through, twisting it so the loop is perpendicular to the first element.

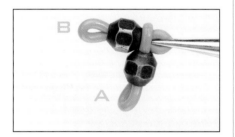

3 Open a jump ring and lace it through one of the black O-rings and then one of the brick red O-rings. Lace the same jump ring through the end of Element B you pulled through. Close the jump ring. Use both flat-nose

pliers for this process and as needed for the following steps (page 16).

4 Insert the round-nose pliers through the free end of Element B, and pull the end of a third element (C) through and twist it, as you did in step 2.

5 Open a jump ring and lace it through a brick red O-ring, a black O-ring, and the free end of the O-ring you just pulled through.

6 Attach a fourth element (D), as shown in the top photo at right. The joined units form a zigzag.

materials + tools

26 yellow O-rings, 12 x 8 x 2 mm

26 brick red O-rings, 7 x 3 x 2 mm

26 black O-rings, 7 x 3 x 2 mm

26 metal beads, 6.5 x 6 mm, with holes large enough to hold a flattened 12-mm O-ring

52 gold 16-gauge anodized aluminum jump rings, ¼ inch

12-inch (30.5 cm) length of 2-ply waxed linen string

Round-nose pliers

Flat-nose pliers, 2 pair

BASIC ELEMENT #1

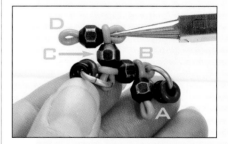

7 Lace an open jump ring through the end of the element you just pulled through. Lace this same jump ring through the nearest attached brick red and black O-rings on the same side of the zigzag, attached to Element B. Close the jump ring.

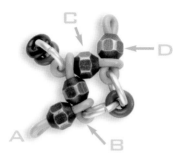

8 Repeat steps 6 and 7 to make another square shape with a fifth element (E). Lace a new jump ring through the end of this element and the nearest attached black and brick red O-rings on the same side (C). Whenever you add two new 7-mm O-rings in the following steps, reverse the color order.

9 Open another jump ring, lace it through a 7-mm O-ring of each color, and the end of Element D, on the opposite side of the zigzag.

10 Attach additional elements until you've joined them all or until the bracelet is the desired length.

11 Insert the round-nose pliers through the end of the last attached element, and pull the end of the first element through.

12 Open a jump ring. Lace it through the end you just pulled through. Lace on two 7-mm O-rings, and close the jump ring.

13 Open a jump ring. Lace it through the two 7-mm O-rings added in step 12, and attach it to the corresponding element.

14 Open two jump rings. Lace them through the ends of the elements shared by a jump ring, as shown by the first photo below. Add a 7-mm O-ring of each color onto each jump ring. Close the jump rings.

15 Open the two remaining jump rings. Lace each one through one of the two elements that have only one jump ring. Lace two 7-mm O-rings onto each jump ring. Close the jump rings. Rotate all of the jump rings to hide the cut ends.

Notes on Suppliers

Usually, you can find the supplies you need for making the projects in Lark books at your local craft supply store, discount mart, home improvement center, or retail shop relevant to the topic of the book. Occasionally, however, you may need to buy materials or tools from specialty suppliers. In order to provide you with the most up-to-date information, we have created a listing of suppliers on our website, which we update on a regular basis. Visit us at www.larkbooks.com, click on "Sources," and then search for the relevant materials. You can also search by book title, vendor, and author name. Additionally, you can search for supply sources located in or near your town by entering your zip code. You will find numerous companies listed, with the web address and/or mailing address and phone number.

Metric Conversion Chart

Inches	Millimeters (mm)
1/16	1.6 mm
1/8	3 mm
3/16	5 mm
1/4	6 mm
5/16	8 mm
3/8	9.5 mm
7/16	11 mm
1/2	13 mm
9/16	14 mm
5/8	16 mm
11/16	17 mm
3/4	19 mm
13/16	21 mm
7/8	22 mm
15/16	24 mm
1	25 mm

Index

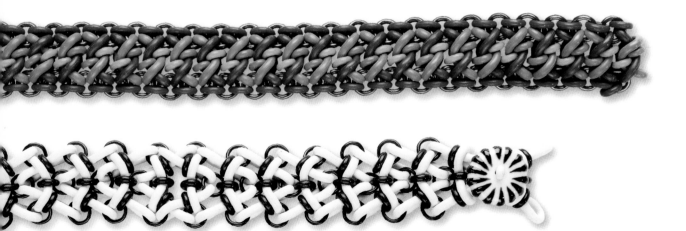